WHEN WE
PRAY
FOR
OTHERS

CARROL JOHNSON SHEWMAKE

When We Pray For Others

The Blessings of Intercessory Prayer

REVIEW AND HERALD® PUBLISHING ASSOCIATION
HAGERSTOWN, MD 21740

This book was
Edited by Gerald Wheeler
Designed by Patricia S. Wegh
Cover design by Mark Bond
Typeset: Minion Reg. 9.5 by 11.5

PRINTED IN U.S.A.

99 98 97 96 95   10 9 8 7 6 5 4 3 2

R&H Cataloging Service
Shewmake, Carrol Johnson, 1927-
   When we pray for others.

   1. Prayer.   I. Title.
         248.32

ISBN 0-8280-0933-3

CONTENTS

TWO QUESTIONS
WITH THE SAME ANSWER

THE GATE OF EDEN was an awesome place. Two bright beings, larger than life, guarded the gate, swinging giant swords from which fire flashed at measured intervals. No human being in his or her right mind would linger here long. Yet it was a singular attraction—the past and the present met at the gate of Eden.

On this day two altars stood in its shadow. On one was heaped a glorious display of fruits and vegetables, while on the other smoldered the remains of an animal sacrifice. Daylight was fast fading, and the shadows of night already enveloped the trees and bushes along the edges of the clearing about the gate, while the gate glowed in the light from the angelic swords.

In the shadows among the trees the figure of a man moved uneasily as he stared intently toward the altars. Only the twittering of birds preparing for night interrupted the uneasy stillness.

Suddenly an authoritative voice spoke out of the quietness.

"Cain," the voice called. "Cain, where is your brother, Abel?"

The man started, looked toward the angels in fear, then upward in anger. "How would I know?" he retorted. *"Am I my brother's keeper?"* Within his heart Cain might well have been saying, "Who am I responsible for, anyway? What obligation do I have for my brother? Isn't my life my own to spend in caring for my own interests? Why live for others? What good will it get me?"

"Cain," God continued, "do you really think that you have hidden your sin against your brother from Me? Since you have taken your brother's life, you will no longer be able to live here among your family and friends. And because you have spilled Abel's blood out upon the earth, the ground will now be twice cursed—once for the sins of your parents, and once again because of your own sin. Cain, you will be a restless wanderer on the earth the rest of your life."

"Are You really going to drive me away from my home and family?" Cain demanded in contempt. "That's too much! I can't bear that kind of punishment. Someone will be sure to kill me!"

"No," God said, "you will not be killed. I will put a mark on you so that no one will dare to kill you without incurring My wrath."

Cain slunk back into the shadows of the trees, gave one last look at the altars, and turned and fled. Skirting the edge of the field where the dead body of his brother lay, he set off at a half run into the night.

God did not answer Cain's impertinent question, "Am I my brother's keeper?" The man was in no condition to listen to God's response anyway. His question was really self-justification of his action. Cain knew that the close tie of brother and sister marked an inescapable obligation, but he chose to ignore it. God had given the responsibility of caring for one another to all humanity. In all of God's beautiful creation, even after the advent of sin, nothing lived unto itself. Every creature, flower, plant, and tree existed for the sake of others. The sun shone in order that plant and animal life might live and grow. The dew sprang up to water the earth. Every creature and plant played its part in life on the earth.

But to human beings God had given a very special role.

"I give you and your family this whole earth and everything in it," God had told Cain's parents as He presented the newly completed earth to them. "This is all yours to use, look after, and care for. Fill this earth with your children and their children. I give it and all its inhabitants into your care. This is your responsibility." Sin alone had marred the perfect plan. Human beings now turned inward in self-interest rather than outward in caring responsibility for God's creation.

A later prophet observed that "there is nothing, save the selfish heart of man, that lives unto itself" (*The Desire of Ages,* p. 20).

No man or woman lives alone. We all have a responsibility to those around us. Oh, it's true, Cain, you were not your brother's *keeper*, if that means to *coerce* him. Human beings have never received the charge to *control* those around them. But Cain, you were to have loved him as you loved yourself. Instead of taking his life from him, you were to have guarded it with your own. His safety should have been secure in your presence.

To each of us God has given the ministry of loving each other as Christ loves us. Jesus told His disciples just before His crucifixion: "A new commandment I give you: Love one another. As I have loved you, so you must love one another. By this all men will know that you are my disciples, if you love one another" (John 13:34, 35).

Luke 10 tells the story of the lawyer who tried to trick Jesus into saying something that some of the Jewish leaders could use against Him. He asked Jesus, "What must I do to inherit eternal life?" Jesus chose to answer his question with another question.

"What does the law say?" He asked.

The lawyer quoted from the books of Deuteronomy and Leviticus as he answered: " 'Love the Lord your God with all your heart and with all your soul and with all your strength and with all your mind,' and, 'Love your neighbor as yourself' " (Luke 10:27).

" 'You have answered correctly,' Jesus replied. 'Do this and you will live' " (verse 28).

The shrewd lawyer then asked, *"Who is my neighbor?"* Like Cain, he sought to justify his lack of love for those he disagreed with. Jesus replied to his question with one of His best-loved parables, the story of the good Samaritan. In it Jesus answered Cain's question—as well as the lawyer's query—with the same answer: we are to show concern and love for our brother and sister and our neighbor. And our neighbor—or brother or sister—is anyone who touches our personal world.

Like Cain and like the lawyer, I sometimes have trouble with my relationships with other human beings. I have also asked myself, What responsibility do I have to those around me? Can I nurture and care for myself and my immediate family, and shut out the rest of the world and its needs? When the Bible says "Love your neighbor as yourself," does that really include the whole world?

Am I my brother's keeper?

Chapter One

THE ULTIMATE PRAYER

CAIN AND THE SHREWD LAWYER, told about in Luke 10, were not asking honest questions. They didn't really care what God or Jesus answered, having already made their minds up.

"Am I my brother's keeper?" was Cain's flippant way of saying he wasn't really responsible for his brother.

"Who is my neighbor?" was a similar question. The lawyer cared not a whit how Jesus answered. To him only the Jews were his neighbors. And he was selective even among them.

But you and I—we have some honest questions. We really wonder about these things.

As a Christian, why am I here?

What about prayer—does God intervene in the lives of others when I pray for them? Is intercession important?

Is it possible that through intercession I can really make a difference in my world?

What should be my greatest purpose in life?

Are hours spent in prayer the best use of my time? Would not others be better off if I spent that time working in some humanitarian way?

I have written three books telling you of my adventures in prayer: *Practical Pointers to Personal Prayer* (1989), *Sanctuary Secrets to Personal Prayer* (1990), and *Sensing His Presence, Hearing His Voice* (1994). They mainly zeroed in on having a personal relationship with God and getting to know Him as Saviour from sin, as Father, as Lover, and as Friend. I can vouch for the reality of the experiences I have told you about in these books, how Christ actually invaded my life and is still changing me.

But in this book I'm stepping out—away from prayers for myself. I'm entering another realm: intercession for family, friends, neighbors, governors, presidents, kings—the whole world.

I remember hearing a young man once remark that intercession for others was the ultimate in prayer. At the time I objected, feeling that the remark was highly pious. Daily battling in prayer for myself, I was at that moment barely able to keep from going under in a great crisis in my life. Of course, I prayed for my family, too, but my greatest concern at the time was for myself.

But I know now that the young man was right. Christ is eagerly educating Christians to join Him in interceding for the world. One of our problems is that we easily become discouraged if we don't see immediate answers. We pray vaguely, spasmodically, and with no real direction or faith. In this book I'll share with you some of the things I have come to understand—why intercession is important, what steps are necessary in order to prepare for intercessory prayer, how to pray intelligent prayers for others, how to recognize answers to prayer, and how to organize intercession into a worthwhile and rewarding ministry. I'll not only relate personal experiences but also the conclusions and experiences of others. God does not work in exactly the same way in all of our lives. We differ in personality, life styles, nationality, work, education, and background, and God deals with each of us individually.

Only recently have I been able to fit together the puzzle pieces I have picked up along the way and produce a clear picture. Not complete, of course. There's always room to fit in another piece and gain a better picture. But I am beginning to see the beauty of the picture and more clearly understand the place and value of intercessory prayer.

When my children entered their teenage years and began experimenting with their own ideas of lifestyle, I felt a desperate need to reach into their lives and direct them away from the pitfalls facing them on every side. But I couldn't reach them. They wouldn't listen.

So what is a mother to do? (This question is now a humorous joke in our family, often repeated by our grown-up children. And they all know that what *this mother* does is pray!)

But I felt nothing humorous about my dilemma at the time as I faced four teenagers bound to try their own ways. I felt I was losing my family. This crisis forced me to reevaluate intercessory prayer. Of course, I had always prayed for my children daily—just as I prayed for the colporteurs and the missionaries. But now I began to wonder if prayer for anyone except myself really worked. And I even wondered how real my own relationship with God was. It was at this time that I began my serious search for an *everyday, moment-by-moment* relationship with God. My three books on prayer chronicle this search.

But God did not leave me comfortless in my immediate problems with my children as I sped along my personal journey. He gave me hope as I began to pray more intensely. God invites us to begin praying for others as soon as we recognize its importance. We do not have to wait until we have studied the whole subject through and fulfilled the prerequisites as we would for a college class. In the recognition itself that God desires us to pray for others, He *gives* us the necessary faith to begin our ministry. From the first moment that we catch just a glimpse of God's plan of intercession, we must begin *practicing* it. The story of the demoniacs of Gadera illustrates this point. Newly delivered from demonic control, the men had no idea of the prerequisites for witnessing. Yet Jesus sent them out to witness with no further training. They were given enough *faith* to begin witnessing. And as they practiced witnessing they grew in understanding. The same thing happens in intercession—at least that's the ideal. What often happens in reality is that we fall into a rut, praying ritually for others, and cease to grow in understanding.

When in tears I confronted God about the condition of my children and their needs, repenting at the same time of my own lukewarmness and lack of faith, God stepped in and gave me the faith to get started both in praying for myself and in believing that He would, in fact, hear and answer my prayers for my children.

As I began to pray with more urgency for my children, I asked God to show me how intercession works. Perhaps you may consider this a presumptuous prayer. The fact that God has told us to pray for others should have been enough for me without having to know why. But it seemed to me at that moment in time that if I just had a faint clue as to how prayer for others could possibly be effective, then I could have the faith to pray. You see, I had read that prayer does not change God but changes only me. So how could that help my children, except, perhaps, to make me more loving and caring, and give me wisdom? But in that case it would be much better to just pray for myself in the first place!

And what about people I don't know and will never have any contact with, such as missionaries, the president of the United States, and other world leaders. I can never influence them by my godliness, for I will never meet them. So why waste time by praying for them? Unless—unless *God can do something in their lives through my prayers that He could not do if I did not pray! And this something God can do has nothing to do with my physical presence!* Beginning to get excited as I thought about it, I asked God for confirmation that intercessory prayer does work. The Lord then impressed upon me that He has created all human beings to be interdependent upon one another. Each person has a God-given line of influence through which he or she can touch every other human being, not physically or materially, but through the medium of prayer.

God has purposely limited Himself in His intervention in human lives in order to preserve individual freedom. Otherwise Satan would accuse Him of *forcing* people to serve Him. But in God's plan, when the righteous pray for family, friends, and *even those they will never personally contact,* God then freely acts in the lives of those people in a way that He would not if we did not pray.

God led me to understand this at a time when I needed so much to have the faith to pray for my children. Within the next few years I saw three of my children choose Christianity as their lifestyle and begin their personal journey toward intimacy in a relationship with God. The fourth—along with a dearly loved foster son—has still not made that permanent choice. But my prayers for all my children remain constant. I know God is at work in their lives, and *my prayers are aiding Him in that work.*

Catching a glimpse of the importance of intercessory prayer might make one decide that it is the *only* prayer we need to pray. But praying for a personal relationship with God is of first importance as we follow the steps of repentance and confession, ask for the Holy Spirit, and walk in obedience. All parts of our relationship with God can grow together, just as a child learns to walk and talk and care for himself or herself all at the same time.

However, there should come a time in our lives as growing Christians when we live consistently in intimacy with God, have confidence in our salvation, and can devote the majority of our prayer time to intercession. It is then that we can develop intercession into ministry. The biographies of great men and women of God, such as John Hyde, missionary to India; George Müller, builder of orphanages; Rees Howell, powerful intercessor; and others whose prayers changed the world—all provide examples of the type of Christian we should long to be.

Is intercession a gift of the Spirit, along with teaching and preaching, given only to select men and women who then become powerful in prayer? No. The ability to intercede with God for others is a gift available to every born-again Christian. In fact, it is our *calling*, the ministry God has given each of us.

"Nothing delights Him [Jesus] more than to find those whom He can take with Him into the Father's presence, whom He can clothe with power to pray down God's blessings on those around them, whom He can train to be His fellow workers in the intercession by which the kingdom is to be revealed on earth" (Andrew Murray, *Ministry of Intercession,* p. 5).

SUMMARY

Does God intervene in the lives of others when I pray for them? Is intercession important?

We find the answer as we consider God's plan for humanity. God created all of us to be interdependent upon each other. Each human being has a line of influence through which he or she can touch every other human being, not physically or materially, but through the medium of prayer.

God has purposefully limited Himself in intervention in human lives in order to preserve individual freedom. Otherwise Satan would accuse Him of *forcing* people to serve Him. In God's plan, when the righteous pray for family, friends, and even those they will never contact, He freely acts in the lives of those people in a way that He would not if we did not pray.

Although praying for a personal relationship with God is always of first importance, intercession for others should accompany even our very first prayers for ourselves. God intends that all parts of our relationship with Him should grow together.

The time should come in the life of the growing Christian when we have so settled into a relationship with Him that we can devote the majority of our prayer time to intercession for others.

The ability to intercede with God for others is a gift God gives to every born-again Christian. In fact, it is our calling, the ministry God has in mind for every one of us.

Chapter Two

BIRTHPLACE
OF INTERCESSION

L ET'S IMAGINE A SCENE in heaven back before earth time had begun. God the Son is rapidly approaching God the Father, a spring in His step, a joyous gleam in His eyes.

"Father," He calls, "I have such a good idea! You'll love it!"

"Yes," replies the Father, smiling in anticipation, "tell Me about this idea."

"Well, it's just this. Why don't We create another world?"

The Father starts to speak, but pauses as the Son is so eager to continue. "Go on. Tell Me more," He says.

"I was just thinking," the Son explains. "We could make this new world a lesson book for the entire universe. You know how hard it is for the angels to comprehend the unity between You and Me and the Holy Spirit—well, We could create the beings on this new world as much like Us as it is possible for a created being to be. We'll make them in Our image. And as the angels watch them, they can better understand Us."

"Yes, yes!" the Father agrees.

"We can even make them so that they group together in families and endow them with the ability to reproduce their own kind."

"A good idea," the Father comments.

"We'll let them govern their own world, daily asking Us for wisdom, strength, and guidance. And We'll give them complete freedom of choice, just as We have the rest of Our creation," the Son continues. A sad look passes across the Father's face and repeats itself on the face of the Son.

"A great risk," murmurs the Father.

"But worth it," the Son declares.

"Yes," says the Father, a faraway look still on His face.

"Well, what do You think?" prompts the Son.

The Father smiles at the Son. "You know what I think," He answers. "Don't We always think the same? It's a great idea. And You're right; it'll give the angels a new glimpse at understanding Us."

The Father and the Son stand quietly together for a few moments.

"It's so easy to ask You for things," the Son confides. "You're always so interested and supportive."

"My Son," the Father replies, placing His arm around the shoulder of the Son, "I love having You come to Me with Your requests, because *nothing gives Me greater pleasure than to give You what You ask for!*"

Of course, it didn't happen just like that. The Bible tells us that human beings cannot comprehend the thoughts of God. And yet, wasn't it *something* like that? The Son always petitioning, the Father always giving? Intercession began in heaven and continues there as Jesus, our high priest, intercedes with His Father on our behalf.

God the Father, God the Son, and God the Holy Spirit *did* create that new world. And it has been the lesson book of the universe. It *was* risky business creating humanity with freedom of choice, just as the Father warned. But the end result for the universe will make the long struggle worth it all. Not only have the angels and the inhabitants of other worlds learned valuable lessons about what God is like from viewing our little world, but we humans, who yielded to temptation and sinned, are continually allowed to take part with God in a practical demonstration of how God works as we intercede with heaven for blessings on earth.

Before He created the earth, God planned to let humanity govern its own world. That was the instruction that God gave Adam and Eve after He completed His creation. And even though sin vastly complicated the picture, yet God left His original plan in force. The Son of God, through faith, immediately became the Son of man and took Adam's place as earth's ruler, finalizing this exchange at the cross.

Few of us realize the power that the transfer gives us in prayer. As sons and daughters of God we can freely intercede for others—and even the world itself—knowing that if we pray under the direction of the Holy Spirit, our prayers will make a difference. The Father will delight to answer our prayers just as He does those of Jesus, our elder brother.

✗Few of us have ever really caught more than a faint glimpse of God's plan for blessing the entire world through the prayers of Christians. Yes, God *does* send the rain and the sunshine to bless the entire world—without our prayers. But He *does not* bestow spiritual blessings unless we ask Him for them. That is part of His original plan to include humanity in His holy work. We each are to have a part in blessing each other and the world. The Holy Spirit comes only in response to the prayers of believers. When we hear of the mighty working of the Holy Spirit in revival in various parts of the world, it is not happenstance or just that God has gotten around in His timing to bless that portion of the world. No, it is a blessing poured out in response to the specific prayers of Christians around the world who have learned to intercede in behalf of God's work in those lands.

Many Christians have the idea that as the salt of the earth all we have to do is live a good moral life and others will be blessed just by contact with us. But it is more than that. We are to *permeate* the world through our prayers. The thought of such responsibility could overwhelm us except for the fact that the Holy Spirit Himself will reveal to us what and whom we should pray for. He will even give us the words to say! And when we pray under the guidance of the Holy Spirit we can be confident that God *will answer* our prayers. Perhaps not just as we might expect them to be, but God will always answer in His own perfect way.

One Sabbath a speaker at our church mentioned that prayer was for our personal benefit alone, that God had no need of our prayers in order to accomplish any of His work. His statement fomented in my mind for years. I strongly object to being assigned "busywork." To this day I still remember having to write "I will not whisper during school hours" (or some such phrase) 500 times. My husband tells me that during boarding school days he once had to move a large pile of rocks from one spot to another and then haul them back, rock by rock, to the place where they had originally been. Busywork! I felt sure that God, with His perfect knowledge, would be able to find something better than busywork either to punish or to teach His children. Teachers or parents assign busywork instead of profitable labor only out of frustration when they can think of nothing else to do. But God knows what will really help us.

Of course, it may be that I misunderstood the man who spoke in our church. Perhaps he didn't mean it the way I heard it. An Ellen White statement has led many to come to his same conclusion. She says: "Prayer is not to work any change in God; it is to bring us into harmony with God" *(Christ's Object Lessons,* p. 143).

Here she says that we cannot change God's mind by our prayers. But what our prayers can do is bring our minds into harmony with His mind so that we can pray in His will. When we read the entire chapter ("Asking to Give") from which this statement comes we then understand that even when we are praying for ourselves we should always keep in mind that the blessings we ask for ourselves are so we can then give to others. Jesus spent hours, often the whole night, in prayer to His Father, seeking wisdom, strength, and healing to give to others. That is our work too.

One of my original misunderstandings was that God would always use *me* to answer the prayers I prayed. But that was being self-centered! God has many agencies by which to answer prayer: the Holy Spirit, angels, fellow human beings, providential circumstances. Often He uses a combination of agencies. I can always rest assured that He knows and chooses the very best and surest way to answer my prayers. He is not limited to using me just because I was the one who prayed! When I began to realize this I was able to trust God more fully to answer my prayers without trying to fulfill them myself.

God *needs* our prayers to aid in His work, not because He is not powerful enough without us, but because He has *voluntarily* limited Himself to allow humanity to participate in the salvation of the world. That is part of His eternal plan.

No, I am positive that God never assigns busywork. The only prayers that are busywork are rote prayers that do not come from the heart. And they have no value whatsoever! The reality is that intercession is the *ministry* that God has given each of us. And intercession allows Him to bless the world in ways that He could not if we did not pray. Our prayers can change the lives of others, purify Christian ministry, and change the world.

Intercessory prayer turns every personal blessing received into a blessing for others. I have a problem with compliments and praise. Oh, don't misunderstand me; I *love* receiving them! I tend to store those sweet little tidbits away in my mind and bring them out later to enjoy again in secret. In the past I liked to think that God allowed me to receive that praise to help increase my self-worth. But then I began to notice that it didn't work that way. All it did was make me desire more praise! Like a drug addiction, it began to take more and more praise to make me feel good. When I realized that, I confessed my pride to the Lord and tried to avoid compliments or forget them immediately. But then my awkward acceptance of praise often made the people who had sincerely complimented me uncomfortable. When I tried verbally turning everything into praise to God instead of me, I tended to sound pious! And I often wondered if perhaps I was only fooling myself by outwardly handing them over to God but inwardly accepting them for myself.

In my devotional reading one morning I discovered something beautiful. The Bible text was from 2 Samuel 23:13-17: the story of David and his men in battle with the Philistines. The Philistines had captured Bethlehem, and David and his men had holed up in a stronghold among the rocks. Evidently David's army had either a limited water supply or at least the stored water left something to be desired in taste. The story says that David began to be thirsty.

"Oh, that someone would get me a drink of water from the well near the gate of Bethlehem!" (verse 15), David fantasized, never dreaming that anyone would take him seriously. But David was first in the eyes and hearts of his followers, and they longed to fulfill his desire. Three of David's men broke through the Philistine lines and obtained water from the well outside the gate of Bethlehem. Bringing it back, they presented it to David.

When David accepted the water and realized the great risk those men had taken to get it for him, he poured it out on the ground before the Lord rather than satisfy his personal thirst.

This story puzzled me in the past. I felt that David had almost insulted those men by not drinking the water when they had risked their lives to get it for him. But this time I caught a glimpse of the reasoning behind his action. He did not throw it away, but poured it out *before the Lord.* In other words, he used it to make a *drink offering* to God. He recognized that the loyalty and love that led men to risk their lives in order to bring him his gift of water was a holy love, too holy for a human being to accept, but worthy of offering to God.

Any praise, friendship, or love that others give me is too holy for me to accept for my own personal pleasure. But I can pour it out as a drink offering before the Lord and bless more lives than just mine.

Listen to what Oswald Chambers has to say about this:

"What has been like water from the well of Bethlehem to you recently—love, friendship, spiritual blessing? Then at the peril of your soul, you take it to satisfy yourself. If you do, you cannot pour it out before the Lord. You can never sanctify to God that with which you long to satisfy yourself. If you satisfy yourself with a blessing from God, it will corrupt you; you must sacrifice it, pour it out, do with it what common sense says is an absurd waste.

"How am I to pour out unto the Lord natural love or spiritual blessing? In one way only—in the determination of my mind. There are certain acts of other people which one could never accept if one did not know God, because it is not within human power to repay them. But immediately I say—this is too great and worthy for me, it is not meant for a human being at all, I must pour it out unto the Lord, then these things pour out in rivers of living water all around. Until I do pour these things out before the Lord, they endanger those I love as well as myself because they will turn to lust. We can be lustful in things which are not sordid and vile. Love has to get to its transfiguration point of being poured out unto the Lord" (*My Utmost for His Highest*, p. 247).

Instead of hoarding praise to satisfy myself, I can immediately pour it out in a drink offering to the Lord, letting it well over into a flowing spring that creates rivers of water to bless others! What an opportunity! All this morning as I have gone about my daily work I have been mentally pouring out drink offerings to the Lord of all the things I cherish, the many blessings God has given me in the ministry of writing and speaking, of special friendships. I poured them all out before the Lord. No longer need I feel hesitant to recall these special blessings, for I am no longer hoarding them to pleasure myself, but have presented them as offerings to God. And He, in turn, will take them and turn them into blessings for those for whom I pray.

The ministry of intercession is truly the ultimate prayer. When we realize that God has made Himself dependent upon the prayers of Christians to bless the world, we can then turn in joy to eagerly intercede for the souls of men and women and the support of the ministry of preaching and teaching. All God gives to us He has purchased with the life blood of His Son. As we pour out these blessings as a drink offering to God, we in fact are giving God permission to bless our world through us. Not all are summoned to be teachers and preachers, but we are all called to be intercessors. The birthplace of intercessory prayer is in the heart of God. If every church member were an active intercessor, how quickly we could finish God's mission on earth, and Jesus could come to complete His salvation.

THE ULTIMATE PRAYER

My great need arose before me,
        and I bowed before the Lord
            in tears.
I found words to express my need
        and strung them out
        before the Lord,
                over and over and over again.

I cried and wept and spent hours in prayer.
Every day, day after day,
        I repeated my needs,
        repented of my sin,
        and received forgiveness.

One day I sensed the monotony of
        my prayers.
There's more—more—more
        to talk to God about than this,
        I decided.

"Go on," God whispered, "go on—
        I've just been waiting
        for you to discover
        the world out there
        with its needs.
        Talk to Me about the hungry,
        the homeless, the unsaved.
        Talk to Me about your family,
        your friends, your church.

"I have no other way to reach them

but through your prayers.
That has always been My plan.
Trust yourself in My hands
and reach out to the world.

"I delight to answer prayer.
    I've been answering yours
    for your personal redemption.
    Now reach out farther still
    and pray
        the ultimate prayer."

SUMMARY

Intercession had its birthplace in heaven—the Son of God asking, the Father giving.

It was always God's plan to let humanity govern their own world. Even though sin complicated the picture, yet God left His original plan in force. Although He sends the sunshine and the rain to bless the entire world without our prayers, He bestows spiritual blessings only if we ask for them. We are to have a part in blessing each other and the world. The Holy Spirit comes only in response to the prayers of believers. When revival sweeps any part of our world, it is in response to the prayers of those believers around the world who have learned to intercede in behalf of God's work.

Christians are not to bless the world just by living in the world—we are to permeate the world through our prayers. The Holy Spirit will reveal to us what and whom we should pray for. He will even give us the words to say. When we pray under the guidance of the Holy Spirit we can be confident that God will answer in His own perfect way.

Prayer does not change God; prayer brings our minds into harmony with His so that we can pray in His will. The Lord has many agencies He uses in answering our prayers: the Holy Spirit, angels, fellow human beings, providential circumstances.

God *needs* our prayers to aid in His work, not because of insufficient power on His part, but because He has voluntarily limited Himself to protect individual free will and to allow the human race to participate in the salvation of the world. God does not assign prayer either as punishment or as a device to teach us. True prayer is a ministry that allows God to bless the world in ways He would not if we did not pray. Our prayers can change the lives of others, purify Christian ministry, and change the world.

Whenever we receive compliments, praise, or material or spiritual blessings, if instead of grasping them to ourselves we immediately realize that we are not worthy of these blessings but God is, and if we consciously offer them in our minds to the Lord as a drink offering, then He will use them to bless the world. God will take them to help those for whom we intercede.

Chapter Three

IT'S ALL IN
THE RELATIONSHIP

THE OLD TESTAMENT WRITERS use five different illustra-
tions to describe the intimacy with God that we can have: a
ruler God and His obedient people; a shepherd and his sheep;
a husband and his wife; a potter and the clay; and a father and his
children. All such comparisons help us to understand the relationship
that God desires to establish and maintain with His people.
Considering all the metaphors used in the Old Testament, perhaps we
find ourselves most drawn to the calls like these: "As a father has
compassion on his children, so the Lord has compassion on those
who fear him; for he knows how we are formed, he remembers that
we are dust" (Ps. 103:13, 14). " 'How gladly would I treat you like
sons and give you a desirable land, the most beautiful inheritance of
any nation.' I thought that you would call me 'Father' and not turn
away from following me" (Jer. 3:19).

Although the Old Testament reiterates the father-son relationship
throughout its pages, yet we do not find any of the recorded Old
Testament prayers beginning "Our Father." Abraham, friend of God,
did not call God "Father." Scripture records neither David nor
Solomon as addressing Him as "Father." Although the Old Testament
freely used the metaphor of God as Father to illustrate the relationship
of God with faithful human beings, yet it almost seems as though it
never occurred to any of them that they could actually *call* God Father.

But the New Testament reveals that Jesus came to earth and *lived*
out the father-son relationship. Boldly Jesus prayed, "My Father."
And Jesus teaches us how to pray to our Father. Again and again He
tells us how much the Father delights to have us acknowledge Him as
our Father by coming to Him with our requests and petitions. It's al-

most as though He is saying, "This is what a Father is for—to *give*, to answer prayer."

Ellen White, in speaking of God as our Father, says:

"In order to strengthen our confidence in God, Christ teaches us to address Him by a new name, a name entwined with the dearest associations of the human heart. He gives us the privilege of calling the infinite God our Father. This name, spoken to Him and of Him, is a sign of our love and trust toward Him, and a pledge of His regard and relationship to us. Spoken when asking His favor or blessing, it is as music in His ears. That we might not think it presumption to call Him by this name, He has repeated it again and again. He desires us to become familiar with the appellation" (*Christ's Object Lessons*, pp. 141, 142).

The New Testament calls Jesus, as He embarked on His earth rescue mission, "the only begotten of the Father" and "God's only Son." Until His resurrection, that is. Then He became the "first begotten"— the first of many children, our Older Brother. We too are God's dear sons and daughters.

The other afternoon I was scrubbing the tile counter in my kitchen vigorously, musing meanwhile on some areas in my life that just seemed impossible for me to keep right with God—the plague spots in my character. While I say I was musing, I was really crying on the inside, weeping at how I so often dishonored God by my thoughts and feelings—and sometimes even actions. The occupation of scrubbing the dirt from the grout between the tiles aptly portrayed what I wanted done in my life.

"Oh, God," I wept as I scrubbed away, "will I ever learn? Whatever do You think of me?"

I don't believe that I really expected God to answer that question, because I was astonished when my spiritual ears caught His answer.

"Carrol," He said, "you are My beloved daughter in whom I am well pleased."

I was amazed! In spite of my struggles—and often falling—God still called me His beloved daughter and He *was pleased with me.* How could that be? He surely wasn't pleased with my failures! I tried to think of what in the world He could possibly be pleased with about me. Finally I decided that it was my turning to Him for help, my dependence upon Him, my willingness to try again. I remembered that "he knows how we are formed, he remembers that we are dust" (Ps. 103:14).

"The word that was spoken to Jesus at the Jordan, 'This is my beloved Son, in whom I am well pleased,' embraces humanity. God spoke to Jesus as our representative. With all our sins and weaknesses, we are not cast aside as worthless. 'He hath made us accepted in the Beloved' (Eph. 1: 6). The glory that rested upon Christ is a pledge of the love of God for us. It tells us of the power of prayer—how the human voice may reach the ear of God, and our petitions find acceptance in the courts of heaven. By sin, earth was cut off from heaven, and alienated from its communion; but Jesus has connected it again with the sphere of glory. His love has encircled man, and reached the highest heaven. The light which fell from the open portals upon the head of our Saviour will fall upon us as we pray for help to resist temptation. The voice which spoke to Jesus says to every believing soul, This is My beloved child, in whom I am well pleased" *(The Desire of Ages,* p. 113).

It is only within the framework of this acceptance as God's dearly beloved sons and daughters that we are able to minister as intercessors. Andrew Murray, apostle of prayer, says this:

"There is a twofold use of prayer: the one, to obtain strength and blessing for our own life; the other, the higher, the true glory of prayer, for which Christ has taken us into His fellowship and teaching, is intercession, where prayer is the royal power a child of God exercises in heaven on behalf of others and even of the kingdom" *(The Ministry of Intercession,* p. 52).

Just as Jesus revealed boldness in approaching His Father, so can we when we accept the concept that we are *dearly loved children.* Children have a freedom of access into their fathers' presence that is completely natural and uninhibited. They can innocently approach him at all times. I remember so clearly the photographs of the oval office of the president of the United States during the term of John F. Kennedy, with Caroline or John-John playing contentedly under or around the desk while the president worked. The children apparently felt no awe for the great man their father was in the eyes of the people of the United States. He was only their dear familiar father, and they did not hesitate to bring to him their childish joys and complaints. They played freely in his presence.

When we gain that same confidence with our Father we can boldly present before Him not only our own needs but those of our family, friends, and the world.

In the first chapter I listed five areas in which God has been teaching me about intercessory prayer. The first one, *why intercession is important*, I discussed in the second chapter and hope that each succeeding chapter will enlarge our understanding of its importance. The second area, *the steps necessary to prepare for intercessory prayer*, I will discuss in the next few chapters. The last three areas, *how to pray intelligent prayers for others, how to recognize answers to prayer,* and *how to organize intercession into a worthwhile and rewarding ministry,* I will discuss in the remainder of the book.

Although God hears and answers the most amazingly simple prayers, yet we always need to learn more about prayer. It is futile to continue offering routine prayers on and on if you secretly doubt that God ever answers any of them. It may even be that you do not allow yourself to doubt, but hold on with what you believe to be faith, continuing to pray your set prayers, yet seldom seeing an answer or sensing joy in your prayer life. Or you may find praying burdensome and tedious and pray little. In those cases it would be well to investigate prayer, find out what pleases God in prayer, and discover what conditions He has placed upon hearing and answering our prayers. It may be that many of our prayers never reach the ear of God at all—not because He doesn't want to listen to them, but because in our lives and attitudes we have made it impossible for Him to respond to them as they are! We need to understand how to approach God so that He can respond to us. Ellen White exhorts us to study into the *science of prayer (Christ's Object Lessons,* p. 142). This suggests that we can *learn to pray better prayers!*

The basic preparation for intercession is the Father-son or Father-daughter relationship with God. Jesus explained it to Nicodemus as being "born again." This is essential to any prayer life. But *God hears and answers any honest prayer.* You don't need to know anything, not even the name of God, surely not a list of conditions, in order for God to answer your prayer if you come in honesty and repentance, believing in the existence of an all-powerful being.

Yet God plans for us to grow as we come to know Him better. To expect Him to answer our prayers when we carelessly ignore the conditions He has clearly stated in His Word is surely presumption. But unless I know God *intimately* I may not recognize that I have not fulfilled the conditions, even though I have walked with Him for a long time! So that leaves me in a dilemma. It's almost a vicious circle—I can't receive answers to my prayers because I haven't fulfilled the conditions, and I can't fulfill the conditions because I don't have an intimate relationship with God. It was exactly this problem that started me on my search for intimacy with God that culminated in my writing my first three books on prayer.

I found the solution in the study of the wilderness sanctuary. When I realized that God gave the Old Testament sanctuary to God's people to illustrate how He saves each human being, I began to seek to cooperate with Him in my personal salvation by using the steps that the priests took daily in their sanctuary service as a guide for my morning prayers. These seven steps led me into an intimacy with God in which I could honestly evaluate whether I was fulfilling His conditions for hearing and answering prayer.

They have also prepared me for a special ministry in intercession. The seven steps include:

1. Praise to God, my Creator, as I enter His courts.

2. Repentance and confession at the altar of sacrifice.

3. Daily cleansing, emptying of self and sin, and rebaptism at the laver.

4. Daily infilling of the Holy Spirit at the lampstand.

5. Spiritual food for growth, obedience, and action at the table of shewbread.

6. Intercessory prayer for others at the altar of incense.

7. Meeting the judgment that involves investigation, discipline, and instruction in the Most Holy Place.

You will notice that if I daily follow each step, they will preserve me in the Father-daughter relationship with God that promotes intimacy. Exposing any cherished or ignorant sin, they keep me Spirit-filled and enable me to respond to Him in obedience and action. The seven steps also include daily intercessory prayer at the altar of incense. As I intercede for others in prayer, I participate in the judgment work of Christ as He serves in the Most Holy Place in heaven as our high priest.

I have included intercession in my daily prayers since childhood. My earliest prayers always ended with "Bless Mother and Daddy and my sisters." Sometimes they included aunts and uncles and cousins, grandma, and perhaps even the pets. And of course, the missionaries and the colporteurs. I seldom left them out. But I had no idea that my prayers for others were really important. Or that God expected me to work on my relationship with all the people I prayed for. I don't suppose that any child has that kind of comprehension.

As the years passed, though, my understanding of prayer grew. But my intercessory prayers were still mainly rote. Except for those for my children. As I reached into my heart and pulled out prayers for them, I never dreamed that it was the Holy Spirit who gave me those prayers.

When I began following sanctuary prayer and came to the altar of incense, it was as though God stopped me and said, "You'll need to make a few changes in the way you pray for people."

"In what way?" I wanted to know.

"Well, there are a few things you need to realize. For instance, when you ask Me to work in the life of someone you personally dislike, I can't answer that prayer. You see, your heart and your words disagree, and I have to have agreement between your mouth and your heart."

"Do You mean, Father, that I shouldn't pray for the people I don't like? They surely need Your help."

"There's another solution to the problem," God said with laughter in His voice.

"That if I would *like* them, then I could pray for them?"

"That's the idea," God replied.

"But I *can't* like them; I really can't!" I exclaimed. "Look what they did to me! They don't deserve my liking them."

"What about forgiveness?" God asked.

"I've already tried that," I remarked bitterly. "But I can't seem to work up forgiveness."

"You're right," God said. "You can't 'work up' forgiveness. Forgiveness is not an emotion, but a choice. When you make the *choice* to forgive those you feel have sinned against you, no matter what they have done, you will be able to forgive them. Of course, that is also the choice to lay aside your bitterness and resentment."

"You mean that all I have to do is to *say* I forgive them?" I asked.

"If you will remember how much I have forgiven you, it makes it easier," God suggested. "Yes, verbalizing forgiveness is important in the act of forgiveness."

"Do I have to tell them I forgive them? Some of them don't even know I hold anything against them!" I was aghast at the enormity of forgiveness.

"My child," God counseled, "the Holy Spirit will reveal that to you. Your first step is the *choice* to forgive."

As I pondered the concept of forgiveness, it seemed as though I discovered references to it in everything I picked up to read! Corrie Ten Boom tells the story of speaking in a church in Germany after the close of World War II. The Nazis had imprisoned her and nearly her entire family in concentration camps for protecting Jews during the time of the German occupation of Holland. Both her father and her sister had died in prison because of the inhuman treatment of their captors.

Corrie had experienced God's amazing forgiveness and felt called to preach that same forgiveness. But it was her first trip to Germany since the war. As she stood at the door after the service, shaking the hands of the people, she looked up and saw coming toward her one of the most cruel of the prison guards, the one whom she deemed responsible for her sister's death. A big smile wreathed his face as he hurried toward her with his hand outstretched.

"Praise the Lord, sister," he called. "As you said, God has buried my sins in the bottom of the sea!"

Unconsciously Corrie put her hand behind her back. *I can't, I can't shake his hand,* she thought.

But instantly she remembered that God had forgiven her and the depths of His love for His enemies. Thrusting out her hand, she said, "Yes, brother, our sins are in the bottom of the sea." She hadn't *felt* forgiveness until she had verbalized it, but the moment she spoke words of friendship, God's love flowed through her to this new brother in Christ.

In her book *Tramp for the Lord,* she says, "Forgiveness is not an emotion. . . . It is an act of the will" (p. 55). What a lesson for me! The things I often harbor against others are so petty when I measure them against real suffering.

Jeff Harkins, in his book *Grace Plus Nothing* (Wheaton, Ill.: Tyndale House Publishers, 1992), tells of his conversion and call to the ministry. But before he could work for others, he had first to learn to forgive. He tells of having the Lord bring to his mind more than 100 people toward whom he held resentments. Harkins says that he verbalized forgiveness for each person, some of them several times.

To verbalize that forgiveness, he used the following formula: "In Jesus' name, because He forgives me, I choose to forgive so-and-so (plug in the name of the individual or group). I hereby cancel their debt. Henceforth they owe me nothing; they never have to apologize; they never have to admit they were wrong. They never have to admit I was right. I let them off the hook. I cancel their debt. They owe me nothing" (pp. 189, 190).

I relate both Corrie's and Jeff's stories in my sanctuary prayer seminars because I have discovered that the inability to forgive is one of the greatest hindrances preventing people from developing an intimate relationship with God. It also keeps them from the ministry of intercession, since they cannot truly pray for people they have not forgiven.

In one seminar I was giving, an elderly woman was sitting near the back of the church as I began. Every now and then she would edge up a row or two, until she was sitting on the front row and cupping her ear with her hand. Although I was using a microphone, she seemed to be having a hard time understanding me. As I tried speaking clearer and louder and directing my voice toward her, I worried that she wasn't getting much out of the seminar even though she seemed intent upon it. As I related Corrie's and Jeff's stories, her face brightened and she seemed excited. Then I told the audience that if any of them wanted to come forward at the close of the meeting I would be happy to let them copy from my notes Jeff's formula for verbalizing forgiveness.

She was the first one by my side. "This is going to change my life," she confided with a bright smile. "There's this woman that I haven't known what to do about. Now I know how to forgive her." She copied the forgiveness prayer, and I pray that it did change not only her life but those of her family as well as the woman she wanted to forgive.

But even when we verbalize forgiveness, it is often hard to really take hold of it and make it stick in our minds. That is why we often must forgive again and again—verbalizing each time. An important part of true forgiveness is the willingness to bear the hurt and pain that person caused us and never mention it again—something that simply isn't easy to do. Perhaps the person we are forgiving has stolen our reputation or sinned against us in a way that caused us to lose years of our lives. But there seems no way that we can *forget* that!

"Forgiving is not forgetting. People who try to forgive by forgetting offenses suffered usually fail on both counts. We often say that God has forgotten our sins (Heb. 10:17). But God is omniscient, so even He cannot forget. Rather, He separates Himself from our confessed and forgiven sin by determining never to use it against us (Ps. 103:12). You can forgive without forgetting" (Neil T. Anderson, *Victory Over the Darkness* [Regal Books, 1990], pp. 201, 202).

What forgiveness involves is that instead of forgetting we resolve to live with the consequences of another person's sin. We really have no choice in the matter whether we forgive them or not. Very few sins against us can be undone. But with forgiveness we make the choice to *bear* the burden of their sin.

"This means that you will not retaliate in the future by using the information about their sin against them (Luke 6:27-34; Prov. 17:9). All true forgiveness is substitutionary as Christ's forgiveness of us was" (*ibid.*, p. 204).

Probably you are thinking that it sounds difficult. But *in Christ* all things are possible. When you *will* to forgive, God will give you true forgiveness. Yet often when the hurt is very deep, you must verbalize it again and again.

If you have a problem with forgiving, I suggest you purchase Neil Anderson's *Victory Over the Darkness* and read especially the section entitled "Healing Emotional Wounds From Your Past." He gives 12 simple steps to forgiveness that you will find exceptionally helpful.

But God wasn't through with me personally regarding intercession. He nudged me a bit more.

"You have a problem with judging people," He said. I had suspected as much, but I didn't really know what to do about it. Two Bible texts had long bothered me:

"Do not judge, or you too will be judged. For in the same way you judge others, you will be judged, and with the measure you use, it will be measured to you" (Matt. 7:1).

"You, therefore, have no excuse, you who pass judgment on someone else, for at whatever point you judge the other, you are condemning yourself, because you who pass judgment do the same things" (Rom. 2:1).

"I just don't understand what those verses mean," I complained, "especially that verse in Romans. How can I help but *see* obvious sin in someone else? Just because I notice when someone has a problem with immorality, or drinking, or jealousy, or anything else, surely can't mean that I have that same problem. Do You mean that I should shut my eyes and just condone their sin? Isn't it normal for a Christian to recognize sin in others and abhor it?"

"Would you like Me to give you a way to test yourself to see if you are judging the person, or if you are just abhorring sin?" God asked.

"Oh, please do," I begged.

"If when you see sin in another's life you feel disgust, anger, or hatred toward that other person, you had better remind yourself of Romans 2:1 and look into your own life for some form of the same sin. For if you truly abhor sin, you will react as Jesus did—with pity, love, and compassion. This is a true test."

I gulped. It was a scary test. But I would use it because I truly wanted to become like Jesus. And I wanted to be an intercessor.

"I don't want you to condone or overlook sin in anyone," God continued. "But when you see sin in someone's life, it is a call for you to pray earnestly for them."

What an opportunity! And what a responsibility for the children of God.

God prodded me some more.

"How can you pray for someone you are criticizing to your friends?" God asked. "Don't you realize that your words *against* them and your prayers *for* them cancel each other out?"

I was amazed, but when I thought about it, it was obvious. I remembered the Bible verse: "May the words of my mouth and the meditation of my heart be pleasing in your sight, O Lord, my Rock and my Redeemer" (Ps. 19:14).

"Another thing," God added. "Prayer must be followed by willingness to become involved with the person you are praying for, if God so wills it."

"Whew," I breathed, "Lord, that will surely keep me from praying for some people."

The Lord eyed me intently. "Even if it is My will for you to pray for them?" He asked softly. "You must keep in mind that all true prayer is put in your heart by the Holy Spirit. Are you really saying that you would refuse to pray for someone I asked you to pray for just because you're afraid I'll ask you to become involved with them in person?"

I hung my head. Perhaps I had meant that. But no longer. It was my desire to please God and do His work at all personal cost to me.

"Forgive me, Father," I petitioned. "Help me to love others as You love them."

"Much better." God smiled.

"Teach me, oh, teach me more about intercession," I pleaded.

"I will," He answered. "Every day I'll teach you more." And He has.

SUMMARY

It is only within the framework of acceptance as God's dearly beloved sons and daughters that human beings are able to minister as intercessors.

In the life of Jesus we see the Father-Son relationship lived out in a human life. Jesus boldly approached the Father in intercession for humanity. A child has a natural and uninhibited freedom of access into his or her father's presence. In the same way we can approach God in prayer when we are confident of our identity as a child of God—a confidence gained through the born-again experience. The seven steps of the sanctuary reveal the way to maintain daily intimacy with God.

1. Praise to God, my Creator, as I enter His courts.

2. Repentance and confession at the altar of sacrifice.

3. Daily cleansing, emptying of self and sin, and rebaptism at the laver.

4. Daily infilling of the Holy Spirit at the lampstand.

5. Spiritual food for growth, obedience, and action at the table of shewbread.

6. Intercessory prayer for others at the altar of incense.

7. Meeting the judgment, which involves investigation, discipline, and instruction in the Most Holy Place.

Followed daily, the seven steps will keep me in the Father-daughter relationship with God that promotes intimacy. They expose any cherished or ignorant sin and keep me Spirit-filled. Besides enabling me for obedience and action, they include daily intercessory prayer at the altar of incense. As I intercede I participate with the judgment work of Christ as He serves in the heavenly Most Holy Place.

Personal lessons God has taught me about intercession:

1. I can't pray true prayers for a person I dislike or hold something against. My words must agree with my heart.

2. Forgiveness of those whom I hold grudges against is a prerequisite for intercessory prayer. Forgiveness is a choice that we can verbalize even though we may not feel the emotion.

Sample of a verbalized forgiveness prayer:

"In Jesus' name, because He forgives me, I choose to forgive so-and-so (plug in the name of the individual or group). I hereby cancel their debt. Henceforth they owe me nothing; they never have to apologize; they never have to admit they were wrong. They never have to admit I was right. I let them off the hook. I cancel their debt. They owe me nothing" (Jeff Harkins, *Grace Plus Nothing,* pp. 189, 190).

At the same time I choose to forgive I must choose also to give up bitterness and resentment, and be willing to *bear* the consequences of the other person's sin against me and thus to never bring it up against them again.

3. When I see obvious sin in someone else, my response should be to pray for them with pity and love. If I feel disgust, hatred, or anger toward that person, I should look for some form of the same sin in myself.

4. I cannot pray for someone I am criticizing to others. Remember, the words of my mouth and my heart must correspond.

5. I must be willing to become involved with the people I am praying for if God so wills it.

Because we are His children, God is willing to teach us more about intercession every day.

Chapter Four

CALLED TO BE A PRIEST

I REALLY HAD NO PLANS to write this book. In fact, when I received notification that the publisher had accepted my manuscript on how to cultivate hearing the voice of God, I heaved a big sigh of relief and decided that that would be my last book! After all, I already had two published books still in the bookstores, and this would make a third. Why not stop while I was ahead? I had spent at least two years writing and rewriting a manuscript on the judgment, a message that I felt was vital but that the publishers thought was either controversial or boring. The rejection had blunted my eagerness to write. But I dared not stop writing altogether while it seemed I had failed, or it would likely color the rest of my life. Now I could safely quit both writing and giving seminars while I was still a winner!

"This is my last book," I told my husband. "I'm going to quit both writing and giving seminars while I'm ahead." He raised his eyebrows and smiled.

"Really truly," I added for emphasis.

For the next three days I immersed myself in my hobby of doll restoration and dressing, planning to accomplish great things. I have a little doll shop in an antique mall, where I sell my finished re-creations. With no writing or speaking trips to take up my time, I could really expand. As I began sewing costumes for dolls, my mind almost seemed to take off on its own.

I began thinking about the growing intercessory prayer ministry God had started me on more than a year before. Now I had great plans for it as well as my doll business. Fortunately the two interests fit well together. I could pray as I sewed. I smiled as I thought of God's great kindness in giving me a ministry that I could carry on quietly right in my home—or wherever I chanced to be. It required little traveling, and I didn't need to write books. My life was on an even keel, with no surprises. I could carry on with my prayer ministry until either death or Christ's coming marked its close.

As I sewed lace on tiny sleeves, gathered skirts, fitted bonnets, I began praying.

"Lord, teach me more about intercession. If this is to be my main ministry for the rest of my life, I need to know all about it. Teach me to really care about people as You do, and keep my *desire* to pray alive. Make me hunger and thirst after You, and keep me constantly sensitive to hear Your voice." Pausing, I searched for a pair of doll shoes and socks to complete a costume. "These are just the thing," I decided, snapping the straps of a pair of black leather shoes around a doll's ankles.

Then I resumed praying. "I've talked to You so much, Lord," I said, "about wanting to reveal the fruit of the Spirit in my life—love, joy, peace, patience, goodness, kindness, gentleness, and self-control—and I know these are important. But now I realize that I also have a great need for the sterner virtues—zeal, passion, steadfastness, strength, and courage. I want to represent You in all I do."

As I mused on, half praying, half thinking, I recalled my almost daily prayer: "Lord, help me to have as close a walk with You as it is possible for a human being to have with God." *How was God going to answer that?* I wondered. After all, I surely couldn't see anything spectacular happening in my life. It just seemed to go on in much the usual way.

My thoughts veered. How grateful I was that God had allowed me to share my prayer experiences with so many people through my books and seminars. It had been a delightful way to witness. My books would continue to witness for the Lord while I went on with my doll business and quietly prayed in my home. Retirement would be good.

"You still haven't written a book specifically about intercessory prayer," a vagrant thought interrupted.

"B-but," I stammered, "I've written *three* books about prayer and intimacy with God, and I've surely mentioned intercession in all of them!" Then I remembered that several years ago a friend had urged me to do a book focusing on intercessory prayer. "Believing in the importance of intercession as you do," she had said, "you should surely share your insights with others."

As I went on with my sewing, an outline began unfolding in my mind: how to become an intercessor, called to be priests, the importance of intercession, how to have the confidence to expect answers, how to recognize answers, how to organize prayer lists, when to pray and how to pray, praying for our children, praying for people we don't know (missionaries, government officials, etc.). On and on the list grew: hindrances to intercession—unforgiveness, criticism, cherished sin.

"Wait a minute," I exclaimed in dismay, "this sounds like a book!"

I put my mind to my dressmaking and concentrated on the essentials of costuming dolls of the past. I had enough to do with my doll business without writing another book!

But the first thing I knew, another chapter was formulating in my mind.

"This is ridiculous!" I grunted, switching my mind back into doll gear. But it wouldn't stay there. The book went on practically planning itself as I worked. I began to get excited. "This could really be interesting!" I exclaimed to myself.

That evening as I sank back into the softness of the sectional sofa in our living room, enjoying the fire in the wood stove and the lights as they came on in the valley below us, I sheepishly admitted to my husband that I thought I'd write another book.

He grinned. "I knew you would," he said.

"Well, for three days I thought I wouldn't," I justified myself. "But I really can't imagine life without a book in the works."

You see, although God gave me the ministry of intercession, He didn't give it to me alone. He gave it to all of you, too. But perhaps you don't know it yet. Or you don't realize how important it is or how to get started. So if I can impress these things upon your mind through relating my experiences, it can be a part of my own ministry.

Years ago when God set me to praying in earnest for my children, true faith finally replacing my childishly sentimental "happily ever after" mind-set, the reality began growing in me that God desired to do for our world through prayer much more than His people were already doing. I caught glimpses of this in Scripture and in my meditation. All that hindered Him was our lack of cooperation. I saw that God's inclusive call to the priesthood of believers excluded neither lineage, ethnic heritage, nor sex. Through this priesthood God would be able to fulfill His marvelous desires for the world.

I especially studied the covenant promises God makes to His people. As He described the covenant relationship, He clearly showed obedience to be the characteristic He desired for those He called to be His children. But obedience seemed to be only the beginning. Beyond obedience God gave humanity a very special commission—not greater than obedience, but *within* obedience.

When He chose the descendants of Abraham to be His chosen people He admonished them: "Now if you obey me fully and keep my covenant, then out of all nations you will be my treasured possession. Although the whole earth is mine, you will be for me a *kingdom of priests* and a holy nation" (Ex. 19:5, 6).

The apostle Peter paraphrases this verse, applying it to the Christian church: "But you are a chosen people, a *royal priesthood,* a holy nation, a people belonging to God, that you may declare the praises of him who called you out of darkness into his wonderful light" (1 Peter 2:9).

Earlier in that same chapter Peter urged the newly born Christians to "grow up" in their salvation so that God can build them into a "*holy priesthood.*"

In Revelation 1:6, 7 the apostle John says: "To him who loves us and has freed us from our sins by his blood, and has made us to be *a kingdom and priests* to serve his God and Father—to him be glory and power for ever and ever! Amen."

Then again in Revelation 5:9, 10 John pictures a scene taking place in heaven. The four living creatures and the 24 elders are bowing before the Lamb of God, holding up golden bowls filled with incense (which, John explains, is the prayers of the saints), singing a new song:

"You are worthy to take the scroll
          and to open its seals,
     because you were slain,
          and with your blood you
               purchased men for God
          from every tribe and language and
               people and nation.
     You have made them to be a
          kingdom and priests to
          serve our God,
     and they will reign on the earth."

Clearly God intends that Christians will take the work of the priesthood seriously. Although the earthly temple services with animal sacrifices were no longer valid after the death and resurrection of Jesus, yet Jesus went on to minister in the *real* sanctuary in heaven as our High Priest.

In the Old Testament God had said that ideally *all* the people were to be priests, not just Aaron's descendants. And now the apostles reiterate that same expectation. The priesthood they visualize is obviously not in an earthly temple, but encompasses a duty that we can all perform in conjunction with our great High Priest in heaven. The apostle John calls this *service*. In the earthly sanctuary illustration of the gospel, the priests were devoted to the service of God. They not only offered sacrifices but interceded for the people with God by presenting their *prayers* on the altar of incense before the Most Holy Place, in which God dwelt. It is the work of priesthood that He has given to all Christians—to serve Him single-mindedly and, through prayer, to intercede for the world with God.

I emphasized in chapter 2 that intercession is a heavenly attribute, a part of the relationship between God the Son and God the Father—the Son asking, the Father giving. When the Godhead created our earth They worked intercession into Their plan for rulership of our world, with God the Son as the intermediary. Earth creatures were to ask in partnership with the Son, and the Father would give. Although sin clouded the divine plan, God still went forward with the same design for earth's rulership. Through His plan the Holy Spirit plants within each Christian the desire to pray for God's work, or for individuals or circumstances that need our prayers. When the Christian prays in accord with God's will, God the Father, through God the Son, responds with blessings.

As I wrote about intercession I began to realize that perhaps the safe, quiet little ministry of intercessory prayer that I was planning for my future was not exactly God's entire plan for me. No ministry for God is ever "safe." Service for God is subject to His direction, not my own. And even though intercessory prayer may be invisible to others around me, it has visible results in the world. I cannot make the decision as to how God wants me to work. Sometimes it may be in the limelight, and yet again it may be a quiet life of retirement. I must be as willing to work either way. God is filled with surprises, and a life devoted to His service will never be dull or safe.

Lest I frighten any shy reader from taking up the ministry of intercession because of fear of what God may call him or her to do, I assure you that God never asks us to do anything that He does not empower us to do. He calls each of us to service within the gifts He has given us. The Lord will not ask us to do anything that He has not prepared us to do. And in the end we will find that following God was easier than had we chosen what seems to us the easy way now.

As I contemplated the possible demise of my plan for a quiet retirement, God showed me a few more things about myself.

"Your decision to stop writing and to refuse speaking engagements came from your fear of rejection," God told me. "That decision is simply an escape."

I immediately began arguing with Him.

"Wait a minute," I implored. "You know I love to write! But perhaps I've had my say. Maybe people don't want to hear from me anymore. And I'm willing to speak to any group that is really interested in what I have to say. I just don't like to speak to disinterested people. I'm not an entertainer, You know," I self-righteously contended, "but I love to speak to those who are seriously interested in living for You."

"You mean you want to be *begged* to speak," God commented, "and complimented afterward."

I reeled under that pronouncement.

"What if," God continued, "I asked you to go and speak someplace where *no one* wanted you to come, where *no one* was eager to hear you speak, would you go?"

I gulped. Would I? *Could* I? Surely not without much prayer and the assurance of His presence.

The story of Jonah flashed into my mind, and I could instantly identify with his sudden trip to Joppa, his purchase of passage to Tarshish, and his escape in sleep in the bottom of the ship.

Then I remembered the young Isaiah and his immediate response to the needs of an unseeing, unhearing people: "Here am I, Lord, send me!"

The little boy Samuel responded to the Lord's call, "Speak, Lord, for Your servant hears You." And though just a child, he went to Eli and delivered the message God had entrusted with him.

Moses, a tired, defeated old man, at first argued with God when He called upon him to return to Egypt to rescue the children of Israel. "Moses said to the Lord, 'O Lord, I have never been eloquent, neither in the past nor since you have spoken to your servant. I am slow of speech and tongue.'

"The Lord said to him, 'Who gave man his mouth? Who makes

him deaf or mute? Who gives him sight or makes him blind? Is it not I, the Lord? Now go; I will help you speak and will teach you what to say'" (Ex. 4:10-12).

Moses still argued. "O Lord," he pleaded, "send someone else to do it." At last, when God volunteered to send Moses' brother, Aaron, as spokesperson, Moses agreed to go, thus beginning one of the greatest life experiences told in Scripture.

Could I go if called? Would I? I have no more confidence in myself than Moses had in himself. My fear of rejection is too great. But I remember Christ's counsel to His disciples: "When you are brought before synagogues, rulers and authorities, do not worry about how you will defend yourselves or what you will say, for the Holy Spirit will teach you at that time what you should say" (Luke 12:11, 12).

Surely that same advice would apply to me should God ever call me, as He did Jonah, to go and speak to those who do not want to listen to me. The only reply I can give to God right now is that without Him I can do nothing, but "I can do everything through him who gives me strength" (Phil. 4:13).

But this chapter is not about speaking, preaching, or teaching. Rather, it is about the prayer of a priest. Prayer that brings about results. Prayer that reaches out and touches God, and through God, the world. But in order for me to be able to pray like that I must permit God to direct my life. God had no problem with my prayers as I worked in my doll workroom. I believe He heard them. What He does not desire for me is that I shut myself off in my own little boxed-in room of prayer. True prayer is as open as the sky, with angels constantly coming and going!

When I saw what God was dealing with in my life I became even more eager to be an active member of His priesthood. I wanted to be able to pray with that kind of openness for those He had given me to pray for! I began to see that God was not asking me to abandon my quiet intercessory prayer ministry. Rather, He was purifying it of all the limitations I had unwittingly given it. He was setting me completely free to pray in the Spirit!

"Do you remember your prayer to know Me in as close a way as it is possible for a human to know God?" He asked me one day. "You wondered how I was going to answer it."

"Why, yes," I said, a light dawning in my mind.

"The more you pray for others with urgent desire and trust, the more you will be able to understand Me and the closer will be your walk with Me," God explained. "By calling you to unite with Me in My intercession for the world, I am answering your prayer."

A smile wreathed my face as I realized that it was true. The more I give myself away in prayer for others, the more intimacy I realize in my fellowship with Jesus!

God is calling His remnant people to the priesthood. In this way He can unite ardent Isaiahs, trusting Samuels, bold Peters, loyal Marys, bustling Marthas, and zealous Pauls into the fellowship of prayer to permeate the world with the blessings of God. Individually we may be invisible, but united we can become "a crown of splendor in the Lord's hand, a royal diadem in the hand of your God" (Isa. 62:3).

"They will be called oaks of righteousness, a planting of the Lord for the display of his splendor" (Isa. 61:3).

SUMMARY

God desires to do much more for our world through prayer than we have ever dreamed possible. He will accomplish His plans through the priesthood of believers as they join Jesus in His high priestly role of intercession.

The Holy Spirit plants within each Christian the desire to pray for God's work, or for those individuals or circumstances that need our prayers. When the Christian prays in accord with the will of God, God the Father, through God the Son, responds with blessings.

In order to be a part of the priesthood, we must allow God to direct us, setting aside our preconceived ideas of how we are to serve

Him, as well as our own fear of rejection.

Biblical examples of God calling men to unite with Him in His work of intercession include:

Jonah—the reluctant prophet

Isaiah—the eager prophet

Samuel—the child prophet

Moses—another reluctant prophet

By calling us to unite with Jesus in His high priestly intercession for the world, God brings us into a closer relationship with Him than we had ever dreamed possible.

Chapter Five

PRAYER IS MEANT TO BE ANSWERED

ONE EVENING AS I PREPARED for bed I felt that I had totally wasted my day. Deeply repentant, I asked the Lord to forgive me. While I knew He was always willing to forgive, I sorrowed that I had learned nothing of Him that day. Picking up my Bible, I asked Him to reveal Himself to me in a special way through His Word.

My Bible fell open to Matthew 17:20: "For truly, I say to you, if you have faith as a grain of mustard seed, you will say to this mountain, 'Move from here to there,' and it will move; and nothing will be impossible to you" (RSV).

"O Lord," I said in disappointment, "I already understand that verse. It means that faith is so powerful that, like the atom bomb, a very tiny bit of it can work miracles."

I can almost imagine that God smiled as He answered me.

"My dear Carrol, you're wrong. In fact, just the opposite is true. Because there is *no power* in faith, even a very little bit is ample to produce miracles. You see, the power is not in faith, but wholly in *Me*! A mustard seed of faith is all that is necessary. All you need is that faith that reaches up and connects with *Me*."

Then the Holy Spirit illumined my mind, and I suddenly understood. All we need do is cry out to God, "Lord, I believe; help thou mine unbelief" (Mark 9:24, KJV). Even that sort of weak faith produces miracles because it is not our faith, but our God who is powerful! The only sort of faith we have available is that same mustard seed of faith being constantly exercised. No one need protest lack of faith as an excuse for any lack of miracles in his or her life. God gives everyone a portion of faith, and the slightest fragment of that unused, rusty, dusty faith will produce miracles—not because of its inherent power, but because of *God's* wonderful love and unending power.

However, there is a beautiful difference between what I call *great faith* and *little faith*. Little faith searches frantically here and there for answers to life's problems, and finally in desperation turns to God for the solution. When great faith meets a problem it immediately seeks God as naturally as a flower does the sun.

When God explained this to me, I marveled anew at how much He depends upon each of us. In every step of our salvation He has planned that we will consciously *choose* to cooperate with Him. And in every prayer we offer, for ourselves or for others, He gives us a part. Our part is that of faith, of just choosing to believe in His love and power and putting that choice into words of petition.

We don't even need to try to manufacture faith. Paul clearly tells us that we are all given a "measure of faith" (Rom. 12:3). That is, every person is given the ability to see in nature and the circumstances of their lives the visible presence of a higher power. We believe because God helps us to believe. This tiny seed of faith that He extends to everyone is sufficient to open communication with God.

Of course, this beginning faith is weak and frail, and often breaks its hold on God. But if we feed that faith on the Word of God, it quickly grows. Remember, *faith itself has no power*. The power is in God. All faith does is to act as the connection that enables us to make contact with God, where all power dwells. Yet faith is so important that Jesus clearly specifies it as being necessary in order for Him to answer prayer. Without that connection with God, He cannot answer prayer.

Jesus said to the woman who touched His garment, "Take heart, daughter, . . . your faith has healed you" (Matt. 9:22). And to the Canaanite woman who begged Him to heal her daughter, Jesus said, "Woman, you have great faith! Your request is granted" (Matt. 15:28).

I discuss faith here because we must have strong faith before we can take on the ministry of intercession. It takes great faith to persevere in praying for others in the face of apparent defeat, disinterest, or even opposition.

For us to have the kind of faith that when faced with a problem *immediately* turns to God, we must feed the small measure of faith that He has already given each of us. The apostle Paul tells us how to do that: "Faith comes from hearing the message, and the message is heard through the word of Christ" (Rom. 10:17).

Since Jesus is our example in prayer, both in words and action, we can expect to find that the stories of His life and the lessons He taught will be our greatest aids to building faith. His first recorded sermon tells us a great deal about prayer. He explained *how* to pray—not to impress our fellow human beings, but to communicate with God in a quiet place. He gave us a simple example of how we can word prayer in a way that will bring us into a relationship so that He can respond to us. Also, He told us the importance of forgiving others so that we could receive God's forgiveness (Matt. 6:5-14).

Then He went on to tell us just how sure we can be that God will answer our prayers: "Ask and it will be given to you; seek and you will find; knock and the door will be opened to you. For everyone who asks receives; he who seeks finds; and to him who knocks, the door will be opened. Which of you, if his son asks for bread, will give him a stone? Or if he asks for a fish, will give him a snake? If you, then, though you are evil, know how to give good gifts to your children, how much more will your Father in heaven give good gifts to those who ask him!" (Matt. 7:7-11).

Jesus spoke with such confidence that the people who heard Him recognized an authority lacking among the scribes and other religious leaders. He spent hours in prayer. It was His habit to seek a quiet place apart from the throng every night or early morning to pray. Jesus spoke as a man who had *experienced* what He was talking about.

As the time approached for Him to die, He spoke more and more about prayer: "Again, I tell you that if two of you on earth agree about anything you ask for, it will be done for you by my Father in heaven.

For where two or three come together in my name, there am I with them" (Matt. 18:19, 20).

"If you believe, you will receive whatever you ask for in prayer" (Matt. 21:22).

"And I will do whatever you ask in my name, so that the Son may bring glory to the Father. You may ask me for anything in my name, and I will do it" (John 14:13).

"If you remain in me and my words remain in you, ask whatever you wish, and it will be given you" (John 15:7).

"Then the Father will give you whatever you ask in my name" (verse 16).

"In that day you will no longer ask me anything. I tell you the truth, my Father will give you whatever you ask in my name. Until now you have not asked for anything in my name. Ask and you will receive, and your joy will be complete" (John 16:23, 24).

Jesus had strong faith in His Father. And He wanted to communicate that confidence to His disciples while He was still with them in person so that they could join Him later in the ministry of intercession. As long as Jesus walked daily among His disciples they felt little need of prayer. But now He was leaving them, and He wanted them to understand that God the Father was eager to respond to their prayers.

Much later one of those disciples wrote:

"This is the confidence we have in approaching God: that if we ask anything according to his will, he hears us. And if we know that he hears us—whatever we ask—we know that we have what we asked of him" (1 John 5:14, 15).

John's faith had grown into a deep and abiding trust. I long to have the same great faith the disciples developed as they put the words of Jesus into practice in prayer. Notice these four P's in developing faith: the *promises* of God and *practice* in *prayer,* plus *praise!* Things like this help me to remember! I ask God to write His promises indelibly upon my heart so that I will not doubt His willingness to answer prayer. Every time Satan tries to persuade me that my prayers for others are useless, I remind myself, "My Father *loves* to give good gifts. He *loves* to answer my prayers."

God especially delights to answer the prayers we offer for others. Asking for blessings for others is a Godlike characteristic, and it pleases God to find that trait also revealed in us.

Then why is it, you may ask, that you pray on year after year for loved ones and see no change?

Let's think about that. Jesus Himself prayed for all His disciples. In John 17 Jesus discussed this in His prayer to His Father in which He said that He had been able to keep all His special friends safe except for Judas. Free will is one of the attributes the Godhead endowed in humanity, one of the ways we are like God. We individually choose either to respond to or reject God's call. Our prayers for others do not interfere with their free will. Even though God turns up the heat around them, they still have the freedom to choose or reject. Eleven of the disciples chose to follow Jesus. Judas decided to go his own way.

However, just because we see no change does not necessarily mean that those we are praying for have rejected God. Another of God's wonderful principles of dealing with us is that He gives us *time*. One day with God is as a thousand years, and a thousand years is as a day in His sight. Each of us must have the patience and perseverance to pray on though years may pass, yet *daily* expecting results.

But that does not mean that we must focus only on the future, saying, "Someday God will answer my prayers." The truth is that God is answering us *every day*. Never does anyone utter a sincere prayer but that God doesn't hear and answer. In our humanity we are often unable to see the results. Then one day our prayers may seem to be suddenly answered. But the reality is that God was active, in combination with our prayers, all along. In heaven we will find the results of many of our seemingly unanswered petitions.

Perhaps we need to look at prayer in a new way—that prayer is primarily a *relationship* between God and us. We approach Him, not just to present our list of petitions so that He can honor us by fulfilling them, but to *commune* with Him, to talk things over, to trust Him for the best possible outcome.

Whereas in the past I often questioned why God did not answer all my prayers in just the way I expected Him to, I am now learning to trust Him more completely, not questioning why He doesn't follow all *my* suggestions. Whereas my understanding of events and people is limited, God can clearly see the past, present, and even the future. So why should I complain when He doesn't follow my recommendations? I know He has heard my requests and will take care of the situation in the best way possible, and I can then leave it all up to Him.

That does not make me pray less about people and conditions. God has made each of us to be a part of the network of humanity, to help bear one another's burdens. Prayer, in some special way we cannot understand fully, allows God to do things He could not do if we did not pray. As I said earlier, God is not limited in power, but He has *voluntarily* restricted Himself in order to give humanity complete free will. When I pray, it allows God freedom to work within His plan. So if anything, I pray *more* than in the past. But I am less rigid, less controlling, in my demands. I am learning to trust in the permanence of my *relationship* with God rather than continually testing it by how often He answers my prayers in just the way I expect Him to.

It all boils down to how much we really *believe* that God will answer *every prayer* in some way (either yes or no or wait awhile)—how much we *trust* God to do the loving thing. Reading and rereading the words of Jesus about prayer and then putting those words into practice will dramatically increase our faith. We need to resist doubts and encourage faith—something best done in prayer, in direct conversation with the Father who loves us *so very much.* And in the *name* of Jesus. In fact, we can ask the Father to give us the very faith of Jesus.

I admit that I am often tempted to doubt, that my faith is not as yet great faith. How I admire the great intercessors of the past and today, like Roger Morneau, author of *Incredible Answers to Prayer,* who pray with great faith. But my encouragement comes through knowing that even little faith is able to connect with God and receive answers. And my faith is *growing faith.*

Faith has an identical twin sister! Her name is Obedience. Actually, they are more like Siamese twins, as one cannot exist without the other. Andrew Murray describes the two in this interesting way: "Faith is obedience at home and looking to the Master: obedience is faith going out to do His will" *(With Christ in the School of Prayer,* p. 146). True obedience reveals the inner faith. It has helped me to compare the relationship of faith and obedience to the relationship of Jesus and God. God is invisible to human eyes. Jesus came to make Him visible. Just so, our faith is invisible to others until our good works—or obedience—make it visible. Obedience is the outer manifestation of our inner faith and will always bring glory to God.

Although God always intends that prayer should receive an answer, there are necessarily conditions that must be met in order for God to justly answer. It will help our faith to grow if we understand the conditions so that we can be sure that we have fulfilled them. Jesus began His assurances about prayer with the words "If you believe . . ." Belief—or *faith*—then, is the first condition with *obedience* making it visible. When Jesus said "If you abide in me . . ." He was referring to a continual state of living faith, a life of *faith and obedience.*

Jesus said that if anyone made the decision to do the will of God, He would make that will plain to the person (John 7:17). I saw this fact clearly illustrated when a young man came to live with us for a few months. Al, tall, gangly, and seemingly sincere, had been expelled from college for using drugs. We hoped that a few weeks with us would help him to get his life in focus. He seemed to be continually searching for God's will for his life. One afternoon he flopped down on the floor beside the easy chair in the bedroom where I was reading and began his familiar discussion as to what might be God's will for him.

"Al, if God suddenly showed you His will for you, would you do it?" I idly asked, expecting him, of course, to immediately answer,

"Yes!" But to my surprise he hung his head and pondered. Finally he looked me straight in the face and laughed sheepishly.

"Well," he said, "I'd have to wait and see if it was what I wanted to do."

"Al," I said emphatically, "God doesn't work that way! Until you decide to follow God's will in your life no matter what the consequences, you will never discover it." He unwound his long legs, stood up, shrugged his shoulders, and sauntered off.

The second condition to answered prayer is to *ask "according to His will."* But to ask according to His will, we need to know what the Bible has to say about it. Using the Scriptures as we pray is a powerful tool to build our faith. And as in every other part of the Christian life, God calls for our participation in learning His will.

"Those who decide to do nothing in any line that will displease God will know, after presenting their case before Him, just what course to pursue. And they will receive not only wisdom, but strength. Power for obedience, for service, will be imparted to them, as Christ has promised" *(The Desire of Ages,* p. 668).

George Müller, man of faith, used six steps to ascertain the will of God concerning what he was praying for.

1. He sought to yield his will entirely to God concerning the matter, to be wholly open to receive God's will.

2. He did not leave himself open to feelings or impressions, but guarded himself against delusions.

3. He searched through the Holy Spirit for God's will in Scripture. Careful to always combine the Scriptures and the Holy Spirit, he said, "If the Holy Ghost guides us at all, He will do it according to the Scriptures and never contrary to it."

4. He took into account God's leading in providential events, having found that he often discovered God's will through a combination of the Holy Spirit, the Bible, and circumstances.

5. He spent time in prayer, asking God to make His will plain.

6. Müller commented, "Thus, through prayer to God, the study of

the Word, and reflection, I come to a deliberate judgment according to the best of my ability and knowledge, and if my mind is thus at peace, and continues so after two or three more petitions, I proceed accordingly. In trivial matters, and in transactions involving most important issues, I have found this method always effective" (Taken from A.E.C. Brooks, in *Answers to Prayer From George Müller's Narratives* [Chicago: Moody Press], p. 6).

As you can see, great men of prayer take the måtter of prayer seriously and are willing to spend much time in thought, Bible study, and prayer, seeking to determine God's will. Many of us find this hard to do. We want our prayers premixed just as we find our food on the grocery shelves. It takes retraining our minds to prepare them for true prayer.

The third condition to answered prayer is *persistence:*

"Having asked according to His Word, we should believe His promises and press our petitions with a determination that will not be denied.

"God does not say, Ask once, and you shall receive. He bids us ask. Unwearyingly persist in prayer. The persistent asking brings the petitioner into a more earnest attitude, and gives him an increased desire to receive the things for which he asks" (*Christ's Object Lessons,* p. 145).

Jesus illustrated the importance of perseverance in prayer with a story of a poor man who received unexpected company—a friend who had been traveling all day and was hungry. The culture of his time demanded that he fix supper for the traveling man. And this is just what the poor man wanted to do, but his cupboard was empty! Then he remembered a wealthy friend of his who had plenty. Leaving his wife to entertain the guest, the poor man rushed to the rich friend's house and knocked on the door, calling out the rich man's name.

"Lend me some bread, friend," he called. "I have unexpected company, and he is hungry. My cupboard is empty. Give me some of yours so that I can feed my friend."

"Go away," the rich man replied, "we're already in bed." (Because even wealthy families in New Testament times all slept on mats in one room, he could not get up without stumbling over and disturbing his sleeping family.)

But the poor man would not leave. It was unthinkable that a friend of his should come to him in hunger and receive nothing. He continued to pound on the rich man's door, until finally the door opened and the rich man thrust out the bread, grumbling, "Some people just won't take no for an answer!"

"Our prayers are to be as earnest and persistent as was the petition of the needy friend who asked for the loaves at midnight. The more earnestly and steadfastly we ask, the closer will be our spiritual union with Christ. We shall receive increased blessings because we have increased faith" (*ibid.*, p. 146).

Christ's parable has special meaning to intercessors. We are the poor man asking his wealthy friend for food to feed the needy. And God asks for persistence from us, not because He is in bed and we are a nuisance to Him, but because He knows that persistence will develop in us the qualities necessary for intercession. God's response contrasts with that of the rich man in the story. The Lord does not grumble as He gives to us—He smiles!

The fourth condition to answered prayer is to *ask all our prayers in the name of Jesus.* He came to earth as the only begotten Son of God. After His death and resurrection, He ascended to heaven as the first of many brothers and sisters. In His name we receive the righteousness of His holy life, His character. Our prayers become His prayers:

"The prayer of the humble suppliant He presents as His own desire in that soul's behalf. Every sincere prayer is heard in heaven. It may not be fluently expressed; but if the heart is in it, it will ascend to the sanctuary where Jesus ministers, and He will present it to the Father without one awkward, stammering word, beautiful and fragrant with the incense of His own perfection" (*The Desire of Ages,* p. 667).

"The Lord is disappointed when His people place a low estimate upon themselves. He desires His chosen heritage to value themselves according to the price He has placed upon them. God wanted them, else He would not have sent His Son on such an expensive errand to redeem them. He has a use for them, and He is well pleased when they make the very highest demands upon Him, that they may glorify His name. They may expect large things if they have faith in His promises" *(ibid.,* p. 668).

Praying in the name of Jesus places us in the position of a daughter or son of God petitioning his or her Father. The Jews attached great importance to naming their children. Often they gave them names that designated their character traits—or what they desired their characters to become. The name of Jesus represents His character. It denotes all that He is. When we pray in the name of Jesus we are acknowledging Him as Saviour from sin, as omnipotent God, and as loving Father.

The fifth condition to answered prayer is to *pray by the inspiration of the Holy Spirit.* The Holy Spirit prompts all true prayer.

"We must not only pray in Christ's name, but by the inspiration of the Holy Spirit. This explains what is meant when it is said that the Spirit 'maketh intercession for us, with groanings which cannot be uttered' (Rom. 8:26). Such prayer God delights to answer. When with earnestness and intensity we breathe a prayer in the name of Christ, there is in that very intensity a pledge from God that He is about to answer our prayer 'exceeding abundantly above all that we ask or think' (Eph. 3:20)" *(Christ's Object Lessons,* p. 147).

The final condition to answered prayer is perhaps the least understood. *All answered prayer must reveal the glory of God.* This isn't because God's vanity desires to be the center of everything, but rather because God *is* the beginning and the end of all creation. *He is* the center from which all life radiates. The eternal reality is that God is all in all. Prayer that does not center in on this fact is selfish, and He cannot safely answer it. Often when we pray and see no immediate answer, God is saying, "Your petition is granted. Your answer will be visible just as soon as it will bring glory to God." We find numerous biblical examples of this principle. Abraham and Sarah had a son when God's timing was right and the answer brought glory to Him and fitted in with His eternal purpose. Zechariah and Elizabeth and the birth of John the Baptist is another example. The couple had also long petitioned God for a child. As they had passed childbearing age they had given up on ever seeing an answer to their prayer. However, God had already granted their petition and was only waiting to fulfill it when it would most glorify Him. The birth of John the Baptist, forerunner of our Lord, was indeed a glorious answer!

Another familiar example with a more immediate answer is the story of the death of Lazarus. His sisters prayed that Jesus would heal their brother. But it was to God's glory to raise Lazarus from the dead.

We should look beyond our plans and pray that the answers to our prayers will bring God glory.

Briefly stated, the basic conditions to answered prayer are:
1. Faith and obedience
2. Praying according to God's will
3. Persistence in asking
4. Praying in the name of Jesus
5. Praying by inspiration of the Holy Spirit
6. Bringing God glory

Through these simple conditions God has made it easy for us to receive answers to our prayers.

One day as I was thinking about prayer, God led me to realize that true prayer intimately involves four individuals: the human being who is praying; the Holy Spirit who plants the prayer in human hearts; Jesus, our high priest and elder brother, through whom all prayer ascends; and God the Father, who answers the prayers. When I look at prayer like that, it makes my faith grow! All prayer is *God's* initiative. Three fourths of prayer is wholly in His hands, and only one fourth is my responsibility. And the Holy Spirit puts even that one fourth into my heart!

Isn't it obvious by now that when we pray we should *expect* answers? We lose so much by our lack of faith, by not searching out God's will, by asking once and no more, by praying routinely in Jesus' name but not comprehending the position God wants to give us as His beloved children in Jesus, by failing to seek for the Holy Spirit's guidance as we pray, and by overlooking the glorious fact that all answered prayer will reveal God's glory.

"Let your heart break for the longing it has for God, for the living God. The life of Christ has shown what humanity can do by being partaker of the divine nature. *All that Christ received from God we too may have. Then ask and receive.* With the persevering faith of Jacob, with the unyielding persistence of Elijah, claim for yourself all that God has promised" *(Christ's Object Lessons, p. 149; italics supplied).*

SUMMARY

Because faith has *no power* in itself, even a very little bit of faith is enough to produce miracles. It taps into the Source of all power. Faith is simply our connection with God, who has all power. But without that connection our prayers cannot be answered.

Prayer is primarily a *relationship* between God and man. We come to Him to commune with Him, to talk things over, to trust Him for the outcome.

Faith has an identical twin sister—obedience. Faith is never visible until revealed by obedience. Obedience is the outer manifestation of our inner faith and will always bring glory to God.

Briefly stated, the basic conditions to answered prayer are:
1. Faith and obedience
2. Praying according to God's will
3. Persistence in asking
4. Praying in the name of Jesus
5. Praying by inspiration of the Holy Spirit
6. Bringing God glory

True prayer intimately involves four individuals:
1. The human being who is praying
2. The Holy Spirit, who plants the prayer in the person's heart
3. Jesus, our high priest, through whom all prayer ascends
4. God the Father, who answers prayer

All prayer is *God's* initiative. Three fourths of prayer rests wholly in His hands. Only one fourth of prayer is my responsibility. And the Holy Spirit puts even that into my heart!

"All that Christ received from God we too may have. Then ask and receive" (*ibid.*, p. 149).

Prayer is meant to be answered.

Chapter Six

HISTORY OF INTERCESSION

WHEN GOD CREATED THE WORLD and put humanity in charge of all His creation, He gave us the opportunity to participate in miracles. He joined humanity's feeble strength to the incredible might of divinity. And all this just a prayer away!

The mighty men and women of the Bible relied completely upon prayer in every part of their life and work. The apostle Paul, too late a convert to Christianity to personally know Jesus before His death and resurrection, relied not only upon his own prayers to God to guide and protect him in his missionary work, but rested heavily on the intercession of other Christians.

I am convinced that Christians today pray too little and have little faith in the prayers of others in their behalf. We seek too much to stand alone before God, forgetting that God chose us to be a *people,* a crowd of witnesses. Yes, of course God saves each of us individually. But we live collectively. What one of us experiences will in turn affect us all. We need to identify more with one another, to pray earnestly for one another and enlist one another's prayers.

The apostle Paul spoke often of his prayers for others. His primary concern after his conversion on the road to Damascus was for his own people. "I have great sorrow and unceasing anguish in my heart," he said, speaking of his fellow Jews (Rom. 9:2). In fact, Paul goes on to say that he would be willing to be cut off from Christ if that would bring the Jews to accept Jesus! Since he elsewhere said "For to me, to live is Christ" (Phil. 1:21), it shows his exceeding love for his countrymen. He loved them more than he valued his own eternal life and was willing to die eternally if he could make such an exchange! Paul longed for them to know the joy of the Lord.

"My heart's desire and prayer to God for the Israelites," he wrote, "is that they may be saved" (Rom. 10:1). His great love and concern drove him to much prayer. And great sorrow, as he realized that the Jews as a nation had rejected the teachings of Christ. But God blessed Paul by expanding his ministry, sending him as a missionary to the Gentiles. This gave him a whole new scope for intercession.

In writing to the church at Corinth, he said: "I always thank God for you because of his grace given you in Christ Jesus" (1 Cor. 1:4). To the Galatians he wrote that he was in the "pains of childbirth" until Christ would be formed within them (Gal. 4:19). And to the church at Ephesus he wrote that ever since he had heard about their faith in Jesus and their love for all the saints, he had not stopped giving thanks for them and continually remembering them in his prayers (Eph. 1:15, 16). Later in his letter he repeated again his concern for them, saying that he kneels before God the Father to pray that they would be strengthened through the Holy Spirit and that Christ would dwell in their hearts by faith. Then he included this beautiful passage about the love of God:

"And I pray that you, being rooted and established in love, may have power, together with all the saints, to grasp how wide and long and high and deep is the love of Christ, and to know this love that surpasses knowledge—that you may be filled to the measure of all the fullness of God.

"Now to him who is able to do immeasurably more than all we ask or imagine, according to his power that is at work within us, to him be glory in the church and in Christ Jesus throughout all generations, for ever and ever! Amen" (Eph. 3:17-21).

To the Philippians he said: "I thank God every time I remember you. In all my prayers for all of you, I always pray with joy because of your partnership in the gospel from the first day until now" (Phil. 1:3-5). The Colossians received a letter with much the same message (assurance of his love and his prayers), as did the Thessalonians and Philemon. To Timothy, his beloved son in the gospel, he wrote: "Night and day I constantly remember you in my prayers" (2 Tim. 1:3). Often Paul would say, "I make mention of you always in my prayers." The apostle was a man who strongly believed in intercessory prayer. Where did he find the time and the privacy? The truth is that we will find time for the things most important to us. Prayer, for Paul, was of first importance. He was a man who "prayed without ceasing."

Not only did Paul pray for others, but he relied upon their prayers for him! To the church at Rome he wrote: "I urge you, brothers, by our Lord Jesus Christ and by the love of the Spirit, to join me in my struggle by praying to God for me. Pray that I may be rescued from the unbelievers in Judea and that my service in Jerusalem may be acceptable to the saints there, so that by God's will I may come to you with joy and together with you be refreshed" (Rom. 15:30-32).

In his letter to the Ephesians he asked them to pray especially for him that he might be bold and fearless in sharing the gospel (Eph. 6:19). These are just samples of Paul's concern about prayer. He valued intercession, recognizing that it was through prayer that God was able to open doors of ministry to lead men and women to salvation, to comfort, and to instruct.

Up until the advent of Jesus to our world, God's people most often associated prayer with animal sacrifices. The early patriarchs offered up morning and evening sacrifices, combined with prayers for their families and neighbors. By the time Israel set up the sanctuary in the wilderness, they had almost entirely lost the practice through years of captivity in a land that prohibited the open worship of God. Through the sanctuary services, God reinstated morning and evening prayers. As the people smelled the scent of the incense offered by the priest at the altar of incense, they knew that their prayers were ascending heavenward to God. God lost no opportunity to teach His people the practice of prayer.

In the book of Job we read of the patriarch's prayers for his children, each prayer for each child accompanied by an animal sacrifice.

Later when Job's great testing had abated, God required the so-called friends who had provided such perverse comfort in his troubles to ask Job to pray for them. The Bible then comments: "After Job had prayed for his friends, the Lord made him prosperous again and gave him twice as much as he had before" (Job 42:10). By praying for his friends, Job had participated in blessing himself! It always works that way when we sincerely pray for others. We cannot do good to others without having it return to us.

Abraham, known as the father of the faithful, was an intercessor. The Bible lists him as God's friend. But he was also the friend of his fellow human beings. His intense plea to God to preserve Sodom (see Gen. 18:16-33) is a classic in intercession.

Moses, chosen by God to lead His people out of bondage to the Promised Land, was another friend of God. When God's people created and worshiped a golden calf, Moses pleaded with Him to forgive them. He even boldly asked God to strike his name from the book of life if He would not spare the Israelites! God kindly reminded him that "whoever has sinned against me I will blot out of my book" (Ex. 32:33).

But God was not displeased with Moses' boldness. He assured him that He was pleased with him and knew him by name (Ex. 33:17). The Bible observes that "the Lord would speak to Moses face to face, as a man speaks with his friend" (verse 11).

Both Nehemiah and Ezra had an intense concern for the salvation of their people. The Bible records some of their prayers of intercession and tells of the blessings God was able to pour upon His people because of the petitions of the two men.

Countless Christians are still sending the prayers of the shepherd boy David heavenward. His prayers for his people, for his country, and for blessings are still moving the hand of God.

Daniel was another man beloved of God who was an intercessor. His prayer for his exiled people (Dan. 9) is one of our best examples of how to approach God in intercession. It has been the basis for my prayers for my family for many years. I pray for my family as Daniel prayed for his people, confessing our sins as a family and speaking of our need of restoration.

The Bible reveals a continual line of intercession through which God blessed the world. But sometimes He could find no one to pray! Sad, but true.

Isaiah comments: "And he saw that there was no man, and wondered that there was no intercessor" (Isa. 59:16, KJV). "And I looked, and there was none to help; and I wondered that there was none to uphold" (Isa. 63:5, KJV).

Ezekiel adds: "And I sought for a man among them, that should make up the hedge, and stand in the gap before me for the land, that I should not destroy it: but I found none" (Eze. 22:30, KJV).

At times in earth's history God could find no Abraham, Moses, Daniel, or Paul to intercede for His people. These were dark days, indeed, not only for the church but also for the world.

Although the world does not realize it, it is only through the prayers of earnest believers in God that the world is blessed with prosperity and a measure of peace. Without the presence of Christians, God would have long ago destroyed the earth.

The brightest spot in the entire history of earth came just after the darkest period. Although at the time the Old Testament story ends and for the 400 years before the New Testament narrative takes up the Bible story, God's people had at long last given up worshiping the gods of the nations around them, they had still not humbled their hearts before God so that they could be a blessing in the world. Instead, they had drawn their self-righteous robes around them and separated themselves entirely from foreigners and those Jews they deemed sinners. Few true intercessors pleaded before God.

But out of the darkness, the fullness of time brought about the birth of Jesus Christ (Gal. 4:4), and His life lit up the whole universe. The apostle John says that the darkness will never be able to put out that light! Of course, the Son of God has always been our liaison with heaven. But now He comes as one of us, flesh and blood, one of God's creation. His primary purpose was to take our place in death, to save us from our sins. But in doing that He also gave us a perfect example of righteous living and intercession. We see in the Gospels His intense prayers ascending daily to His Father. Could He have been praying only for Himself all those hours? Of course not! He was praying for His disciples, for the priests and rulers, for the multitudes. And He even prayed for you and me.

"My prayer is not for them alone. I pray also for those who will believe in me through their message, that all of them may be one, Father, just as you are in me and I am in you. May they also be in us so that the world may believe that you have sent me" (John 17:20, 21).

Christ died on the cross with a prayer on His lips for those who killed Him. "Father, forgive them," He prayed, "for they do not know what they are doing" (Luke 23:34). Here was intercession of the highest level!

No true prayer is ever lost! Angels record them all, and God answers them again and again. Jesus arose victorious from the grave and ascended to heaven to intercede continually for sinful men and women, never forgetting His humanity or His mission. "Therefore he is able to save completely those who come to God through him, because *he always lives to intercede for them*" (Heb. 7:25).

Christ sits today at the right hand of the Father, His human arm reaching down to us, His divine arm encircling His Father. When we intercede for others, our faith reaches up and makes contact with Jesus, who then adds His prayers to ours, giving ours the power of His holy life.

Too often it takes a long time for spiritual concepts to burst into bloom in my dull human mind. I comprehend a little one day, then a little more another day, and finally, seemingly in a moment of time, I see the beautiful picture. It has been that way about my privileges as a child of God. One privilege I really coveted was to sit with Jesus on His throne.

As I was praying one evening I seemed to see heaven, God on His throne, and thousands of heavenly beings singing, "Holy, holy, holy." It was not a vision—I was perfectly conscious of all around me. Nor was it a dream—I was wide awake. But God planted in my mind a picture as clearly as if I had seen it in physical reality.

From the throne a Voice said, "Carrol, if you were here in heaven, you wouldn't be happy unless you were sitting on My throne with Me so that all eyes would be focused upon you."

I was horrified! Although it is natural for me to be in the center of a group, telling a story, expounding a theory, relating an experience, surely, in my conscious mind, I had never dallied with the idea of competing with God! I enjoy the response of quick laughter, surprise, or common interest to my contribution to the conversation. Now God's words frightened me. Was I really that self-centered? For once I didn't argue with God, but became unnaturally quiet. With humility and a prayer for God's forgiveness and restoration, I murmured, "O Lord, change me!"

Until this moment I had really never planned to tell this story. I am sure you can see why. Besides, I had no idea just where God was going with this disclosure, so I tried to forget about it.

But then a few days ago in my morning prayer time God brought back that memory.

"Oh, no," I cried, "not that again!" And I repented anew of my pride.

But God had more for me this morning than just a reminder of my weakness. He directed me to reread the promise Jesus had given to the overcomer in the church of Laodicea in Revelation 3.

Because I had been so fearful when God first spoke to me about this matter, I had tried to block the experience from my mind instead of seeking to find out just what God was trying to teach me. But He, with the persistence of divinity, was determined that I would open up my mind to what He wanted to show me despite my fear. So I reread God's counsel to Laodicea: "To him who overcomes, I will give the right to sit with me on my throne, just as I overcame and sat down with my Father on his throne" (verse 21).

Filled with awe, I was, for a wonder, speechless!

"Don't you see, Carrol?" God told me. "I don't want you to give up your dream of sitting on My throne. You *will* get to share My throne. But not so that all eyes will be upon you. Oh, no. You will sit with Me because you and I cannot bear to be apart. We will sit together because you, through Jesus, have become an overcomer."

As I sat stunned, God continued, "What's more, by faith you can sit with Me on my throne even now!"

Two passages flooded my mind:

"And God raised us up with Christ and seated us with him in the heavenly realms in Christ Jesus" (Eph. 2:6).

"Since, then, you have been raised with Christ, set your hearts on things above, where Christ is seated at the right hand of God. Set your minds on things above, not on earthly things. For you died, and your life is now hidden with Christ in God. When Christ, who is your life, appears, then you also will appear with him in glory" (Col. 3:1-4).

I began to realize that God has no desire to take away our dreams of Him. But it is necessary that He cleanse them of selfishness and sin.

As an intercessor with Christ for the salvation of lost souls, I can sit with Him in heavenly places even now. And as an intercessor I will weep with Christ in sympathy for the world's sorrow and grieve for its sin.

The prayers of Christians for each other are vital! Ellen White remarks in several places that the weakest saint upon his knees makes Satan tremble. Just what is that "weak saint" praying for? Surely for victory over his own sins. But what is it that makes Satan tremble? Isn't it the fear that as the "weak saint" overcomes his or her own sins that he or she will begin interceding with God for the world? As the "weak saint" begins praying for teachers, leaders, and missionaries—those on the front lines of the offensive campaign to win the world for Christ—Satan trembles because he knows his time is short. More than we do, the devil realizes that those prayers reach the highest throne room of heaven and mean his doom. He knows that the intercessory prayers of weak saints all over the world can mean revival and the blessings of heaven poured out upon individuals, churches, whole regions—and yes, upon the entire world. He knows that one day those prayers will mean his reign of terror is over. Christ and His overcoming saints will rule the world!

SUMMARY

Christians today pray too little and have little faith in the prayers of others in their behalf. We stand too much alone before God, forgetting that He chose us to be a *people,* a crowd of witnesses. Although God saves us individually, we still live collectively. What one of us experiences will affect all the rest of us. We need to identify more with one another, to pray earnestly for one another, and to enlist one another's prayers.

Bible history tells the story of intercession, listing the names of many who interceded with God for individuals and nations: Job, Abraham, Moses, Nehemiah, Ezra, David, Daniel, Isaiah, Ezekiel, Jesus, Paul, and the other apostles.

Sometimes God could find no one to intercede for His people. They were dark times, indeed, for both the church and the world.

It is only through the prayers of dedicated believers in God that the world receives prosperity and a measure of peace. Without the presence of Christians, God would have long ago destroyed the earth.

The birth of Jesus lit up the whole universe, and the darkness of sin will never be able to put out that light. By dying on the cross and rising again to life, Jesus became our high priest, the ultimate intercessor. It is by studying His life and His teachings that we also learn how to become intercessors.

No true prayer ever gets lost! Angels record them all, and God answers them again and again as He sees new opportunities to do so.

The weakest saint upon his knees makes Satan tremble. He knows that eventually such prayers will mean his doom. The prayers of "weak saints" will bring about revival and blessings poured out upon individuals, churches, whole regions—and even the world. Christ and His overcoming saints will rule the world!

Chapter Seven

LEARNING TO LOVE

A MINISTRY IN INTERCESSION usually creeps up on you, born out of an urgent need for help for those you love. Intercession grows in the hearts of those who are themselves developing a personal relationship with God, planted there by the Holy Spirit. It is natural in the Christian life for the one who has experienced the wonderful redemptive qualities of God to desire the same for those they love. Often we do not see it in such a sensible light, however; we begin it in panic and despair.

I speak from experience. It was only as I recognized the desperate need of my children that I saw my own weakness and need. And so intercession for my children began at the same time I set out on the greatest adventure of my life, a new step into intimacy with God. For parents, the most important creatures on earth are their children. Surely this is the place for them to begin the ministry of intercession. For those who are childless, God can use your concern for other family members or close friends, or even the work of God as a whole, to bring you to your knees as you realize your weakness and God's great power.

The insights I am sharing with you about prayer for others did not come to me all at once. So don't despair if you find a problem dealing with some of them at first. Besides, you may not have the same problems that I had. God taught me through the avenue of my concern for my children. He may use a different approach with you.

One of the first things I had to deal with was my dream of myself as the ideal mother. I felt sure that I was the world's best mom. Both my husband and I had devoted our lives to our children. As proof of my saintly motherhood, I could—and I would, if you gave me half a chance—give a list much longer than even the proud Pharisee had put together as he prayed in the Temple. Oh, I was humble enough, just sure that I was a *good* mother. My children came first in my life.

God took that list and showed me what it looked like in His sight. It stunned me. God explained that my love for my children was so contaminated with pride in myself as the ideal mother that genuine love was barely discernable.

My first reaction to what God disclosed was self-pity and abasement. I determined never again to lift up my head, never to speak in public, never to teach another class, never to mention my children to anyone again! I have to laugh now as I think of the trauma I created for myself. Fortunately, my natural good nature and God's sweet acceptance brought me out of my extreme reaction. But again and again God has had to deal with me in a similar way.

My next step was to give my children up to Him completely. We had dedicated each of our children to God as infants. But this was different. I had to give up any plans I had for them, any dreams of their future—and believe me, I had plenty of those! The Lord would not even allow me to daydream about a glorious future for my beautiful, clever children! He blocked my mind every time I began.

Then I had to rebuild love. By this time I had seen my heart in its sinfulness and had not been able to locate any love at all! I was hesitant to even tell my children or my husband that I loved them, so unsure was I of my ability to love. I didn't even tell God I loved Him, although He was first in my affections. In fact, I felt sure that my heart was barren of love.

But God did not leave me long in this loveless state. He opened up a whole new dimension of love to my empty heart. My husband was busily involved in beach evangelism with some college students for the thousands of young people who thronged our small beach city and the beaches around us. The college students were holding evangelistic meetings every Friday and Saturday night in our church. The meetings were unlike any evangelistic series I had ever before attended. Johnny, a young ministerial student with an engaging grin and a guitar, led the song service. After every song or two he would press his right hand flat against the guitar strings to stop the sound abruptly and say "I just can't wait any longer to tell you what Jesus did for me today," or last Wednesday—or whenever. Then he would proceed with a simple story of God's working in his life. Sometimes it was about school, how God helped him to know what to study for a test. Other times it involved his car, an ancient relic that barely got him to the meetings and back. (We eagerly awaited news of that car from night to night. It seemed to run on faith alone.) But often his testimony was about an opportunity the Lord had given him to witness to a fellow student, a service station attendant (because of the old car), or someone else he had met.

As he finished his testimony, he would pause and look around at us and say, "Has God done anything special for you this week?" Of course, He had, so we responded with stories of God's intervention in our lives also. For the first time in my life I was eager to testify. The testimonies of the young people were alive and unusual. I recognized the presence of the Holy Spirit. For me, only one thing disturbed the whole service. One girl who came every night was the first to respond almost each time that Johnny asked, "Has God done anything for you this week?" The problem was that she always said exactly the same thing: "I just want to say tonight that I love Jesus."

Now, you remember that I had become an expert on the human heart. When I examined my own heart I found no love there at all! The human heart had no ability to produce love—of that I was sure. Since I couldn't even be sure of the love I had for my family with whom I lived, how could I possibly say that I loved God whom I had never seen?

I knew that God loved me with a marvelous everlasting love totally unlike my undependable human love, and I rested completely in God's love for me, not in my love for God. But each night that I heard the girl declare that she loved Jesus, I questioned in my mind why she didn't recount some blessing she had received *from* God instead of claiming to be *giving* God something! I grew more and more irritated.

One night when she stood up and said "I just want to say tonight that I love Jesus," I felt I could stand it no longer. I countered inaudibly with "What a hypocrite! How can she say that? How can human love ever be counted as praise by a holy God? Why can't she praise God for blessing her as everyone else does? Why can't she say she's thankful that God loves *her* instead of that *she* loves God?"

Just then an inward Voice spoke to my heated mind. "Carrol," the voice said, "do you believe I love you?"

"Oh, Lord," I responded immediately, "You know I believe You love me. Why, I couldn't exist a single day without Your love! The evidences of Your holy love are around me constantly!"

"Then why," the Voice persisted, "is it so hard for you to take some of the abundant love that I give you and return it to Me? Why do you insist that it is impossible?" The pleading love in that Voice broke my heart. Sudden revelation flooded over me. I had thought I was being conscientious and honest, when in fact I was only being self-righteous and prideful. I wanted to manufacture love myself, when in reality all love comes from God alone.

Instantly I jumped to my feet. At Johnny's nod, I spoke. "I just want to say tonight that I love Jesus."

Looking inward, I had seriously doubted my ability to love others. Looking upward to Jesus, I realized that the only love I had to give was from Him, and He gave freely, enabling me to love freely also. I need not stop to examine my emotions—I could just believe the promise of God and reach out to give what God had already given me.

The ministry of intercession is an experience in learning to love. Our prayers for others are ineffectual unless accompanied by love. But the human heart can never manufacture that love. True love is divine and comes only from the presence of the Holy Spirit in the heart.

When I began to understand this, I realized that I didn't have to search my heart for love for others—all I have to do is ask the Lord to help me *choose* to reach out to them with the love that God has already so freely and constantly given me. It may not always express itself in strong emotional feelings. Love, like forgiveness, is not an emotion, but a principle. We can *choose* to love others without first feeling the emotion, just as we choose forgiveness. We may never have a strong feeling of sentimental love for some people—different personalities attract different people—but we can feel kindly toward them by exercising our God-given power to direct the love God has so freely given us toward them.

Don't misunderstand me in this. This is not make-believe love—not just saying you love while your face and your actions say differently. Although love begins with a choice you make, the love that comes when you make that choice is definitely real. When you choose to love someone, God will supply the feeling and direct your actions to demonstrate that love.

This understanding of love is essential to true intercession. Otherwise, we will hamper our prayers by dishonestly trying to manufacture love ourselves. Satan has a heyday with our ignorance. He may say to me as I am praying for someone to whom I am not naturally attracted: "You know that God requires you to love the person you are praying for. I don't think you love this person. Better forget about praying for him [or her]." While in the past I might have become discouraged at my lack of love and ceased to pray for a particular individual, now I have an answer: "Yes, it's true I'm not naturally attracted to that person, and I have no ability to manufacture love for him [or her], but my heart is so filled with God's love that I have chosen to share that love with this person. I do love him [or her] with the love God has given me." Such a response will get Satan off my back, lighten my conscience, and give me peace. And in that power I can then pray!

Some sincere Christians never grasp the fact that trying to manufacture love only hinders them in expressing it! My parents' generation had a great problem with this. I never heard my father say, "I love you." Yet I know he cared for me. One of the last times I visited my parents' home before my father died, I thought I'd try one more time to get him to tell me he loved me. Mother would take me to the airport for my flight home to southern California. Just before we left, I would walk out into the garden to tell my father goodbye. "I'm going, Dad," I said. "I'll write soon." As I hugged him I whispered, "I love you." Daddy stood still for a moment, then he laughed nervously.

"Well," he said, "I don't really know if I can say I love anyone. It doesn't seem to me that a human being can really love."

My heart was crying, "Oh, Daddy, just say you love me. Please." But he *couldn't* say the words because he didn't realize that no human being can originate love. Love is of divine origin. But we can all freely share the love God showers upon us. In spite of his sincerity and love for God, my father's emotional life was stunted because he had somehow missed this great truth about love.

Yet God used my father to heal our family and knit us together in love for each other and for God. Mother called me when she had to take Dad to the hospital after he had suffered several strokes and she could no longer keep him at home. When I arrived at my parents' home my older sister, Ardith, and her husband, Jim, had been there a week, daily taking Mother to the hospital to see Dad.

In addition to Ardith, who was 22 months older than I was, I had another sister, Opal, who was four years younger. I had bonded to Opal the moment I saw her in the hospital nursery as my dad held me up to look through the round viewing window. I had loved her throughout her life. In my eyes she could do no wrong. But my relationship with Ardith was different. She was a very sensible and conscientious child who tried very hard to please our parents. Accepting responsibility well, she sought to convince me to do the same! Unfortunately, it didn't work. We battled our way through childhood. She left home at 18 to make her own way, and I didn't miss her much. Oh, of course, I *loved* her as a sister, but I felt we had nothing more than that in common. Over the years we kept in touch at Christmas and an occasional visit between our families. But we weren't close. Now and then it bothered me. Surely as a growing

Christian I should have a deeper relationship with my sister. Sometimes I prayed about the situation, but I didn't know how to mend a relationship that had never really bonded in the first place.

But now here we were together while our father was dying. Neither of us had felt close to Dad. He just wasn't the sort you could get emotionally close to. We realized as we visited the hospital that Dad wasn't getting enough to eat, as the nurses didn't have the time it took to feed him. So Mother and the two of us girls began taking turns going at each mealtime to feed Dad. As Ardith and I watched our father grow weaker, as we prayed with him before his meals, and as we fed him, we began to feel differently toward each other and toward him. His weakness made tender love surge up in my heart for him. I caressed his brow— something I would never have thought of doing had he been well.

Together my sister and I watched Daddy die. It was sad and yet strangely sweet. Dad was 83 years old and in declining health. He had loved the Lord and done his best to live a righteous life. Now he was ready to die and not be a burden on his family.

One morning after the funeral, as we finished breakfast at my parents' home, I looked across the table at my sister and realized that she was also very dear to me.

"You know, Ardith," I said, "even if you weren't my sister, you are someone that I would pick out for a friend!" The response in Ardith's face made it plain that she felt the same. As our father died, we had been bonded and our family healed.

Since that time Mother and the three of us have remained very close. Ardith and I often call or write or visit each other. And we enjoy those times together very much. We are vocal in saying "I love you."

God had answered my prayers in, humanly speaking, a most unlikely way. It took a death to heal a family. For not only had Ardith and I been bonded to each other as Daddy died, but we had also been bonded to him. The entire family had been reunited in his death. Both Ardith and I had always been close to Opal, and now we three and Mother walked side by side in love.

As I am writing, this coming Wednesday is my mother's ninety-second birthday. Ardith and Opal will be with her in person to celebrate her birthday, while I will be far away. But whether together in physical proximity or hundreds of miles apart, we are one in the Spirit of love.

Understanding that the only love we have to share is the abundant love God bestows upon us will also show us how to pray for our enemies. Sometimes it almost seems as though God requires us to do the things we cannot do! And it's true that we can't do them of ourselves, but through Jesus we receive power to do everything He asks us to do. But I have found that it really helps to know *how* to do it. Remember the example of little faith and great faith? Little faith rushes around frantically, seeking solutions to life's problems. Great faith immediately turns to God and finds the solution. God delights to share with us the insights that enable us to exercise great faith. "We love because he first loved us" (1 John 4:19).

Loving others is the key to effectual intercession. When we can truly love others, we are free to devote ourselves to prayer for them. We can *practice* love in our thoughts. The thoughts of the Christian who lives in a constant attitude of prayer are prayer itself. So when we indulge ourselves in thinking censorious, judgmental thoughts, resentment, or condemnation, we are using the very channels God has given us for prayer—but for such a different purpose! We have lost our influence for good and have strengthened ourselves in the enemy's tactics. Instead, we need to treat others as we would like to be treated—even in our thoughts. If we see sin in another's life—or what seems like sin to us—let us immediately lift that person up before the Lord in prayer. Let us reach out to him or her, even in our thoughts, with kindness and love.

"Whatsoever is done out of pure love, be it ever so little or contemptible in the sight of men, is wholly fruitful; for God regards more with how much love one worketh than the amount he doeth" (*Testimonies*, vol. 2, p. 135).

SUMMARY

A ministry in intercession begins with an urgent need for those you love. With parents it is for children. Those who are not parents may start from concern for parents, siblings, friends, or the church itself. Although it most often begins in panic and despair, we then need to recognize our weakness and God's great power.

The ministry of intercession is an experience in learning to love. Our prayers for others are ineffectual unless accompanied by love. But we ourselves can never manufacture love.

True love is divine and comes only from the presence of the Holy Spirit in the heart.

It is useless to search our hearts looking for love for others. We will never find it.

All we have to do is *choose* to reach out to them with the love that God has so freely and constantly given us. However, it will not always manifest itself in strong emotional feelings. Love, like forgiveness, is not an emotion, but a principle. We can choose to love others without first feeling the emotion, just as we first choose forgiveness without feeling forgiving. Although we may never have a strong feeling of sentimental love for some people—different personalities attract different people—we can feel kindly toward them by exercising our God-given power to direct the love God has given us toward them.

Such love is not make-believe—not just saying that you love someone while your face and your actions say differently. Although love begins with a choice you make, the love that comes when you make the choice is real love. When you choose to love someone, God will supply the feeling and direct your actions.

Understanding that the only love we have to share is the abundant love God Himself bestows upon us will also show us how to pray for our enemies. "We love because he first loved us" (1 John 4:19).

We should *practice* love in our thoughts, thinking only loving things about people. The Christian in a constant attitude of prayer will find that even his or her thoughts are themselves prayers. So when we indulge ourselves in censoriousness, judgmentalism, resentment, or condemnation, we are misusing the *very channels God has given us for prayer!* It is only when we can truly love others that we are free to devote ourselves to prayer for them.

Loving others is the key to effectual intercession.

Chapter Eight

MINISTRY IN INTERCESSION

TOO OFTEN WE THINK of prayer as "otherworldly," almost fanciful. But in reality, prayer is the essence of humanity, the response of a heart created to worship. God desires us to pray in exactly the language in which we ordinarily speak, not in some mystic spirit language, King James English, special prayer phrases, or unnatural tones. Prayer is to be the honest expression of our hearts, speaking to our Father, our Friend.

When I talk about "ministry in intercession," it may sound a little pretentious, as though it is a big step to take. Actually, most of you are already interceding daily for your family and friends. I always did. But I will admit that, other than for my immediate family, my prayers were rather haphazard—I prayed for people when they happened to come into my mind.

When I began what I call my ministry of intercession I took my intercessory prayers much more seriously and methodically than I had in the past. Although I describe throughout this book how I go about my intercessory praying in order to give you some practical ideas of how it can be done, I am not really suggesting that you must pray the same way. People vary in personality, age, circumstances, and time available. But as I tell you how I do it, perhaps it will start you brainstorming how it might work best for you.

It is important that prayer not become a burden. When prayer turns into a burdensome ritual, it is no longer a blessing to you—and most likely is of little value to anyone else, either. It will sometimes be inconvenient to pray. We all have to sacrifice time and convenience in order to pray. But it need not be a burden if you keep the Holy

Spirit alive in your prayers. True prayer must be the expression of the heart's desire.

I first experimented with intercession in a large way when my husband pastored a church of about 250 members. I was not working away from home at the time and really wanted to be of service to our congregation. I began a women's Bible fellowship that met once a month and enjoyed that. Also, I taught a weekly adult Sabbath school class and faithfully took part in prayer meeting. But I felt the need of doing something more. Our congregation seemed to have such serious needs, and I felt totally inadequate to do counseling. So I decided to pray for the members individually. In order to do this, I divided the names on the church membership list into seven sections, grouping together the families with young children, those with school-age children, retired people, newly baptized, Pathfinder club, etc.

When I was through writing down names, I had seven pages in a spiral stenographic notebook, listed under the days of the week. I kept the notebook standing open on the counter in my kitchen, turned to the appropriate day of the week, and as I passed through the kitchen in my daily work I would stop and pray for one family or one individual on my list for that day, until I had prayed for the entire list. It worked out very nicely as long as we served that congregation. I felt sure that God was using my prayers to bless our church and its members. When my husband changed pastorates, it became necessary for me to go to work outside the home to pay tuition for three children in academy, and I began a job as the school librarian. My days were suddenly so full that the idea of an intercessional ministry slipped away unnoticed. Of course, I didn't stop praying for people. But I did drop my organized prayer list. My prayers were mostly for my children—four teenagers are a mighty responsibility!

My husband began a youth ministry combining students from the nearby Adventist college and the young people crowding our beaches. I was actively involved in that as I led out in Sabbath school, taught a Sabbath school class, and coordinated a weekly Sabbath potluck for all those involved in the beach ministry, plus visitors. My personal prayers centered on developing an intimate relationship with God, while my intercession was for my children and the young people we were working with.

The years passed, and God led me to study the sanctuary, showing me what it reveals about a relationship with God. I became so excited about my discoveries that I wrote books on how to pray and began giving seminars on the same subject. Of course, as I used sanctuary prayer as my personal prayer style, the altar of incense reminded me every morning of the continual intercession of Jesus, my high priest, and I joined Him in praying for those He placed around me.

As I became involved in praying for more and more people, it became necessary for me to write the names down in order to remember them. But as my list grew longer and longer, I began to sense a growing panic as I faced it each morning. *This isn't right,* I thought. *I should pray for these people joyfully, happy to intercede for them.*

A friend of mine who had created a beautiful intercessory prayer ministry and outreach using a day-of-the-week plan continually reminded me how pleasant and convenient it was to pray for people that way. And although I resisted a bit at first, wondering if I really wanted to be as involved as my friend was in intercession, I revamped my list. This time I used my computer and the landscape mode to put the names of the people I pray for, listed by days of the week, into a small 5½" x 8½" booklet. It could be updated when needed and a new copy immediately generated. I found that this size fits neatly in my Bible case with my Bible and is easy to take along with me on trips. And the shorter daily list gave me renewed joy in praying for the people God has entrusted to me!

Some I have talked to tell me that they have no trouble with becoming burdened by too many people on their prayer list as they don't name them one by one in prayer, but just hold up their prayer book and pray for them all collectively. That approach bothers me because I feel that God is calling me to a personal relationship with most of the people He impresses me to pray for. I believe that He will not ask me to pray for more people than I can personally become involved with. True, with some of them my involvement is minimal. I pray for the president of the General Conference, for example. I have never met him, and unless he has chanced to read my articles or books over the years, he has never heard of me. Yet through Christ I do feel that I have a personal relationship with him. We have the same goals, the same basic beliefs, the same urgent desire for the salvation of the world. So I can pray for him with a sense of involvement.

In one way I do pray for people collectively without mentioning individual names. Each morning as I complete praying for the individual people on that day's list, I take my little notebook in my hands and hold it up before the Lord, telling Him that everyone in that notebook is precious in my sight, and I know doubly precious in His. I ask Him to make His presence known that day to all the people listed in my days-of-the-week prayer book. That way I pray for all of my people *every day*, although I usually mention their names only once a week.

I began my special days-of-the-week prayer list in early November, just before preparations for Christmas that year took over my life. For a number of years I have written a Christmas letter that I send to all of our friends and relatives, relating the past year's news. Then besides the general letter I always write a personal note on the Christmas card. This year I especially wanted to have something to say in my letter that would turn hearts toward Christ rather than just having the Shewmake family in the limelight. I prayed about that, hoping to have some brilliant idea strike me before I began the letter. But I had no good ideas, and finally the day came when I *must* write the letter if I was to have it ready to mail in time for people to receive it by Christmas Day. Composing a short letter, I told what we had been doing during the past year. But any idea I could come up with to glorify Christ seemed contrived and trite. So I just left the letter short and unadorned with any special sentiment.

With a sigh I prepared to run the letter off on the copier.

"This isn't really what I had in mind for this year's letter, Lord," I said as I put the original in the copy machine. "But please bless it, that it may in some way glorify Your name."

I ran off 125 copies on green paper and left them on top of my desk along with my boxes of Christmas cards to begin addressing, signing, and writing personal notes the next day.

The next morning during my prayer time, as I was interceding at the altar of incense in my sanctuary prayer, it came to my mind that I should tell the people I had been praying for about my new prayer plan, that I was praying for them on a regular basis, and even what day of the week I especially mentioned their names.

But I had already written my letter, run off copies, and used up all my green paper!

But then I had a sudden thought. Couldn't I run the copies through again, using the back of the letter already copied to add a postscript? I could explain how I pray and then add a personal note at the bottom of the page telling each person which day I pray for them. It was perfect! My problem was solved.

I am including a copy of my postscript, just in case you might like to include a similar note in your next Christmas letter:

"My personal daily prayer list had become so long that it was burdensome to complete it each day. So I was impressed to divide my list into seven sections, one for each day of the week. That way I pray for each of you and your families one day a week. You'd be surprised at how all the burden has been lifted at my shorter daily lists and how I feel real joy as I lift your name up before the Lord. I have asked God to share with me His love for you and to place you upon my heart the entire day that you are on my prayer list.

"I thought that it might be a blessing to you to know the very day that I am praying for you and your family, so I will tell that at the end of this letter. Then, too, I'd like to suggest that you set aside that same day to pray for John and me and our family. That way our hearts will be lifted up *together* to the Lord as we pray for each other.

"This is not a new thing that I am doing. I have prayed this way in the past for our entire church membership. [Of course, I pray *every day* for my husband and children and grandchildren, and for my mother and sisters.] A friend of ours has developed this way of praying into a prayer ministry that is blessing hundreds of people. But it is new for me to pray this way for my family and friends, and it has given my prayers new life. I look forward each morning to praying for the special people God has given me that day to pray for. Sometimes He adds a few names to that day's list—to my surprise!

"I do believe that God has made each of us a part of the network of humanity, to help bear one another's burdens. If I can help bear yours, praise the Lord! I do believe that prayer, in some special way we cannot understand fully, allows God to do things He could not do if we did not pray. Not that God is limited in power, but that He has *voluntarily* limited Himself in order to give humanity complete *free will*. But when I pray, God is set free to work within His plan.

"So feel free to write or call me with special prayer requests. I'd love to hear, too, what God is doing in your life. Let's just bind ourselves ever closer to God and to each other! What a comfort there is in that!

"Love and continual prayers,

"John and Carrol Shewmake"

I received a greater response to that Christmas letter than to any I have ever written! I had included my telephone number so that it would be handy for people to call. And they did!

Since I sent my cards out early in December, many of the people remarked on their own cards about my postscript. "I loved your Christmas letter—especially the PS" was a familiar comment. And many of them said even more.

"I'm going to begin praying that way," more than one wrote. The most moving letter I received was from a simple, childlike woman:

"Your letters warm my heart. It takes a lot of courage to do what you do. I know that it is the Lord's doing. And we are His servants. Nice. I like that. I like being a servant of God. And doing His will. He's my Lord and I'm His servant. I want to walk where He walks ... I'm glad I found a friend in you."

I cannot read that letter even yet without tears coming to my eyes and a feeling of praise to God for His love and blessings welling up in my heart. The honesty and integrity and power of a child of God!

I am hesitant to tell you the next story as I feel that perhaps a door opened for me and I failed to walk through it. But I'll tell it anyway. Perhaps in relating it, God will be able to open my mind to understand where I failed or how I can even yet redeem this relationship.

Joe, the building contractor who framed in our mountain house, was a likable man who quickly became a friend. He and his helper worked hard to build us a charming house that my husband then completed. I never met Joe's wife, but from his conversation I gathered that neither of them were churchgoers—although he believed in God. While his wife smoked, he did not and wished that she would quit. They both drank a little. Her favorite pastime was playing cards. All of this I picked up in conversations with Joe over the months he spent building our house.

When I started to send out my Christmas cards and letters and came to this man's name, I hesitated to enclose my letter with the card. *What will they think?* I wondered. Not knowing if they believed in prayer, I decided to leave out the letter and just send the card. Then God nudged me.

"I understood," He said, "that you were going to include your letter in *every* Christmas card."

"Well, I am," I excused myself. "In every card except this one. It would be rather awkward to send this couple a letter about prayer!"

"Don't you pray for them?" God asked.

"Well, yes, I do. They're on my prayer list. I pray for them every Wednesday."

"Then why not let them know that you pray for them regularly?" God persisted. "I just don't see your problem."

"You think I should?" I asked.

"Most definitely," was the positive response.

So I stuffed my letter inside the card and put it in the mail, sending a prayer with it.

The very next day I received a telephone call. It was from the wife of the contractor.

"I just got your card," she said, tears in her voice. "Joe and I are having such a hard time right now. I just couldn't handle it at all if it weren't for God. Every day after Joe leaves for work I spend time with God in prayer. I have felt so alone. But then I read your letter." She stopped, and I could tell she was having a hard time keeping from crying.

"I never dreamed that anyone else was praying for us!" she exclaimed.

My heart was pounding. By almost not sending her a letter, I had judged her when I didn't even know her!

I murmured something about how I would continue to pray for them and how it would be nice if we could get together someday. As I look back on this incident I know my response was inadequate. I continue to pray for the couple every Wednesday, but I have still never met this lovely and needy woman.

You see, I do believe that intercession includes much more than the act of wording a prayer to God for that person. In chapter 3 I told how God impressed me that when I pray for someone I must also be willing to become personally involved with that individual if He so desires. Sometimes there is no personal contact at all, such as praying for government officials, foreign missionaries, etc. However, I must be open to personal involvement if God ever brings that about or impresses me to take the steps that might create it—such as writing letters, making phone calls, or whatever.

One evening as I was preparing for bed I found myself thinking about this part of intercession. As I knelt for my evening prayer, I asked God to lead me to pray for just the people I should. The name of a woman who had been a member of my husband's last church popped into my mind.

"You don't mean I have to pray for Jess?" I burst out to God, really thinking of personal involvement more than prayer. Hesitantly, and laughing a little, too, I tried to explain to Him just why it didn't seem that I was the person to pray for her. In fact, I decided that perhaps I had only imagined that God had put Jess's name into my mind. (Although I couldn't imagine why I had suddenly thought of her—she hadn't entered my mind for months.) You see, Jess always seemed very uncomfortable in my presence, although I did my best to be friendly. We were such total opposites. Jess was short and wide, gruff, and ill at ease in the church situations I reveled in.

She often attended the Friday night fellowships at our home and especially seemed to enjoy the singing. One evening she told the group that she always felt uneasy at our house, but wasn't sure if it was the house or the people who owned it! Such remarks rather unsettled me. Although I tried to be friendly and to find positive traits in her, it was hard.

And then one year she went along on our annual backpacking trip. There is something about carrying a 40-pound pack up treacherous mountain trails, sitting in the dirt to cook supper, and bathing in an icy river that is a marvelous equalizer. She softened somewhat in her attitude toward me. But we didn't become bosom friends.

And now I was to add her to my prayer list? Although I hadn't seen her for a couple years, I had heard that she seldom attended church anymore.

The next morning in my prayer time I asked God if He had really asked me to pray for Jess or if I had just imagined it. The Lord was silent. But I prayed for her, just to be sure.

I had a dental appointment that morning in Loma Linda and had a hard time finding a place to park my car. Finally I parked in the Loma Linda Market parking lot and hiked the two blocks over to the office. On the way I passed a bench where several people sat waiting for a bus. I blinked in astonishment when I saw that one of them was Jess, reading a paperback as she waited for the bus. Should I disturb her reading? Yes, I should, I decided. This was a simple kind of involvement, and I didn't want to muff it. Greeting her warmly, I asked how things were going. She answered briefly as usual. I doubt that the brief contact had any impact on Jess—but it did on me! Surely this was more than coincidence. I believe that God put Jess in my path that morning to encourage me to trust His leading in my prayer life.

Yes, I had heard God aright. Yes, I will pray for Jess. And yes, I will be willing to become involved with her personally if that is God's will.

Much of my daily praying for others is of necessity mainly "God bless" prayers. I don't know their specific needs, but God does. So I just ask God to bless them according to their needs for that day and to intervene in their lives in just the way that will draw them to Him.

But once in a while God gives me a special Bible promise to claim for an individual or family. When that happens, I jot the text down in my prayer book next to the person's name so that I can use that promise again as God's will for that person's life. When this happens, it gives me confidence that God is working through my prayers. Writing the text down is important, because I believe we often lose the power God wants to give us by not keeping in our memory what He has told us in the past.

For instance, one family I pray for has a number of very conscientious grown children. Satan has attacked several of them in the same way—they feel that Christian leaders have mistreated them. As a result, the family has developed a spirit of despair, resentment, and bitterness, deadly to spiritual growth.

When I began to pray for them, I found myself sinking into their despair. After all, if they had been unjustly treated, it was only right that they should feel resentment! I caught myself in horror. How do you combat such an insidious spirit? Only with the sword of the Spirit, the Word of God. God gave me a Bible text to use each time I pray for them, a verse that radiates hope rather than despair. It is part of the passage from Isaiah 61:1-3 that heralded the mission of Jesus to earth to set the captives free. Verse 3 says that Jesus came to "provide for those who grieve in Zion—to bestow on them a crown of beauty instead of ashes, the oil of gladness instead of mourning, and a garment of praise instead of a spirit of despair. They will be called oaks of righteousness, a planting of the Lord for the display of his splendor."

By rereading this verse each time I pray for this family, I focus on the victory that God wants to give them, rather than partaking of their bitterness. It gives me faith to see this family as radiant, joyful Christians living only to display God's splendor. Instead of pouring sympathy upon people, even in our prayers, let us be channels to receive God's solution to their problems, using the Word of God.

As I urge you to enter wholly into the ministry of intercession I do not pretend to speak as an authority or even from years of experience. I have so much more to learn about being an intercessor! But lack of knowledge need not hinder any of us from beginning this important ministry. God promises to give us knowledge, to supply all our needs. He will teach us *as we step forward to intercede for others.* As I write I am praying that God will use my weakness to strengthen you, to make you mighty in intercession.

SUMMARY

Prayer is the essence of humanity, the response of a heart created to worship. God wants our prayers to be the honest expression of our hearts, speaking to our Father, our Friend, in the way in which we ordinarily speak—no special prayer tone, language, or phrases.

In order to keep prayer from becoming a burden, we need to keep the Holy Spirit alive in our prayers.

Some of the ways I organize intercession into a manageable ministry:

1. I divide my prayer list into seven lists—one for each day of the week.

2. I type my list on my computer, landscape style, making a small booklet 5½" x 8½" in size. Such a size will handily slip in my Bible case to take along on trips, etc.

3. I use this booklet in my morning prayer time, presenting each name on that day's list.

4. When I complete the list, I hold the entire booklet up before the Lord, asking His blessing on everyone in it.

5. As the Lord impresses me with a Bible text or something special that I should pray about for a certain person, I jot that down beside the person's name in my book, to keep it fresh in my mind.

6. Much of my daily praying is of the "God bless" type, asking God to bless them according to their needs for that day, and to intervene in their lives in just the way that will draw them to Him.

7. I focus on the victory that God wants to give each individual. Instead of pouring sympathy upon people, even in our prayers, let us be channels to receive God's solution to their problems, using the Word of God.

Chapter Nine

HOW TO GET STARTED

THE DESIRE TO PRAY enters the heart when one comes to Jesus. No one has to convince anyone that he or she should pray. However, even Jesus taught His disciples *how* to pray. The desire to pray may be in the heart, but sometimes we need guidance in how to pray. God created human beings, not to stand by themselves, but to live for and with each other. The lessons that God teaches us He expects us to share with others. We will be eager to tell others as much as we can about prayer, not because we are authorities on it, but because the little we know may be exactly what someone else needs to hear to make the whole of Christianity real.

Prayer is a personal thing—an intimate relationship between God and human beings. So we should not so structure it that we destroy spontaneity. But in order to understand what is taking place when we pray so that we can recognize answers to prayer, build faith, and make it easier to remember to pray, some order is desirable. In this book we are not discussing the whole of prayer, but just a segment of prayer—actually the highest type of prayer: intercession. Jesus, our example in prayer, asked from His Father in order to give to those around Him. This should also be our ultimate goal—to ask blessings from the Father in order to give them to those around us, not just for blessings for ourselves, or even so that we may be able to work effectively for others, but also that the Lord will give the people we are praying for blessings wholly unrelated to ourselves, a totally unselfish asking and giving. Andrew Murray put it this way:

"When the Spirit of intercession takes full possession of us, all selfishness—of wanting Him separate from His intercession for others and just for ourselves alone—is banished, and we begin to avail ourselves of our wonderful privilege to plead for men. We long to live the Christ-life of self-consuming sacrifice for others. Our heart unceasingly yields itself to God to obtain His blessing for those around us. Intercession then becomes, not an incident or an occasional part of our prayers, but their one great object. Prayer for ourselves then takes its true place as a mere means of preparing us better so that we can be more effective in the exercise of our ministry of intercession" (Andrew Murray, *The Ministry of Intercessory Prayer* [Minneapolis: Bethany House Publishers, 1981], pp. 77, 78).

For those of you who may feel the Holy Spirit calling you to a deeper ministry in intercession but don't quite know how to begin, I would like to dedicate this chapter. It will be somewhat like a news article and deal with the *who, why, what, when, where,* and *how* of intercession. Like a news story, I will try to deal with how to pray intercessory prayer in a very practical way.

WHOM TO PRAY FOR

If you are considering developing a serious ministry in intercession, you need to begin a prayer list. God has given each of us a circle of people for whom we have responsibility: our children, our siblings, our parents. We can extend the circle to relatives, friends, neighbors, and business and social acquaintances. Under God's direction you should formulate your list. It is wise to write it down, as it is all too easy to forget someone if you try relying on memory alone.

Next consider the work of God: your individual church; any special outreach your church sponsors; your pastor; your local conference and its officials; the General Conference headquarters and personnel; and the outreach programs of the world church—evangelism, missionaries, schools, hospitals, publishing houses, colporteurs. Under the direction of the Holy Spirit, choose some specific project and people to pray for.

World leadership is another area to choose from: the president of our country and other leaders; congress, state, and city officials; and rulers of other countries. Perhaps you might pray for the hunger problems of the world, or the problem of violence and war. Here again, don't try to cover the entire country or world with your prayers, but ask God to direct you to the specific areas and people He wants you to pray for.

From these broad areas you will be able to put together your own tentative list. My suggestion is to begin in a small way and be specific. Satan will do all he can to discourage you from intercession, and if your list is long and general, you may begin to feel hopeless. Begin slowly, and as you begin to sense the real blessing in this kind of praying, you can add to your list as God impresses you.

WHY INTERCESSION IS IMPORTANT

It is God's plan to bless the world through the prayers of His people. "Prayer is the greatest resource of the church. It is the most effective means of preparing the way of the Lord available to us as Christians today. You yourself can influence more people for God and have a greater role in advancing Christ's cause by prayer than in any other way. It is not the *only* thing you must do, but it is the *greatest* thing you can do. It has often been said,

" 'The Devil trembles when he sees

God's weakest child upon his knees.'

"If that is true, think what could happen if every Christian really took his prayer role seriously and began to pray regularly and specifically, uniting with thousands or millions of others, all praying for the same priority needs around the world. Are you willing to be a part of such a prayer army?" (Wesley L. Duewel, *Touch the World Through Prayer* [Grand Rapids: Zondervan, 1986]).

Remember, our prayers allow God to do for others what He could not do if we did not pray.

WHAT WE CAN ASK GOD TO DO FOR OTHERS

The easiest type of prayer list is simply a "God bless" list, stating the names and asking God to bless and direct each person that day according to His will. It may be the best way to pray for some of the people you put on your prayer list. But often God will impress you of specific things to pray for or Bible promises to claim for those you are praying for. As I mentioned previously, jot them down next to the name on your list so that you can claim the same promises for them again. When God has given me a special Bible text for someone on my prayer list, it immediately increases my faith. I know that God is interested in my prayers for that person. It gives me the faith to believe that He is actively involved in the life of that person.

One way to know how to pray for someone on your prayer list is to ask that person what they want you to pray for them. In that way you will receive added strength, for there will be at least two people joining in that prayer—you and the other person involved. Jesus said that where two people on earth agree about anything they ask God for, it will be done (see Matt. 18:19).

The apostle Paul was a great intercessor. And he believed in letting the people he was praying for know that he was praying for them. In nearly every one of his letters he told of his prayers for the people. Examining the Epistles of Paul, we can get some ideas of what we can pray for the people on our own prayer lists. His first prayer in each letter seems to be one of thankfulness for their faith, of praise to God for the people themselves. Then he often follows this up with prayers for wisdom, knowledge, and understanding for them so that they can know God better. You may want to study Paul's prayers for ideas for your intercession. Here is one I especially enjoy praying for my children:

"And this is my prayer: that your love may abound more and more in knowledge and depth of insight, so that you may be able to discern what is best and may be pure and blameless until the day of Christ, filled with the fruit of righteousness that comes through Jesus Christ—to the glory and praise of God" (Phil. 1:9-12).

Anything that God promises to give His people would surely be an appropriate prayer: victory over sin, forgiveness of sin, boldness in witness, the fruit of the Spirit, power in prayer, good health, and a sound mind, along with, of course, wisdom, knowledge, and understanding. Salvation is something we desire for everyone on our list. We can also pray for food for the hungry and homes and clothes for the homeless, always remembering to listen for God's call to us, showing us where we can sacrifice to help answer our own prayer. We can pray for students to diligently concentrate on their studies. Or we can pray for career choices, jobs, or the right choice of marriage partners.

Always we must conclude our prayers with "Thy will be done." Only God knows the end from the beginning, and He knows just what is best for each person.

WHEN TO INTERCEDE FOR OTHERS

Since we are discussing a daily intercessory ministry, I'll talk first about when to pray for your prayer list each day. Then we'll discuss special occasions when it is appropriate to pray for individuals on your list. Surely, no one set time of day is holier than any other. If you plan to include intercession in your morning devotional time, then morning is the time for you. But we can approach intercession in various ways. No one can answer for anyone else. In the last chapter I related the story of how I prayed for the entire membership in one congregation my husband pastored. I stood the stenographic notebook containing my daily prayer lists on the kitchen counter and prayed for the people as I passed through the kitchen throughout the day. My present prayer style involves following the steps the priests took in the wilderness sanctuary services as a guide for my prayer. In that prayer the altar of incense is the place and time I use for intercession.

I have a friend who takes his prayer notebook with him in the car and to the office, praying throughout the day for the people on his list. It might be that you'd want to have it by your bed and pray early in the morning before you get up or at night after you have gone to bed. Some people take their list on their morning walk and pray as they go along.

I once read of a man who said that he used the things around him in everyday life to call him to prayer. When he heard a siren—ambulance, fire engine, or police—he immediately prayed for the people involved in the crisis the siren implied. When the telephone rang, he prayed for the person he would meet at the other end of the line. Or when he answered the doorbell, he prayed for the person on the other side of his door. The building in which he had his office had several sets of stairs. He used these rather than the elevator, praying for someone on his prayer list on each step as he went up and down.

We don't want to become so organized that we forget that life changes daily for the people on our prayer list and their needs do too. We should be alert to pray for them on the various important days in their lives. For instance, birthdays are a special time. I offer a special birthday prayer for those on my list whose birthdays I know. Then I pray for them throughout the day.

If you know that any of your people are facing a personal crisis, hold them up continually before the Lord. Seek to be sensitive to God's voice telling you when to pray special prayers for those on your list. Whenever anything in your life reminds you of someone on your list, pray for that person right then.

In your heart, gather together the people God has impressed you to put on your list and often bestow love and concern through prayer upon them as you wait for an appointment, as you rest or exercise, or as you find yourself involved in any occupation during which your mind is free.

WHERE AND HOW TO PRAY FOR THE PEOPLE ON YOUR LIST
Here is another area where your praying can vary greatly. Most likely no two people pray just alike. Some pray on their knees or sitting in a chair. Others pray while walking, in bed, sitting on the floor, or half-kneeling. Others pray with arms held up symbolically to receive the Holy Spirit. The only importance I see in posture is that it should represent humility before God. Whenever we pray in sincerity our hearts are bowed at the footstool of the King of kings.

Some intercede alone, while others have a family prayer list and the whole family gathers together to pray. One missionary family I knew made a scrapbook of pictures of the people on their prayer list so that even the youngest child could freely join in the prayers. Prayers of intercession can mix with prayers of adoration or thanksgiving.

I read of one group of friends who have banded together to pray for the schools their children attend. To make the prayers more meaningful in their minds, they meet early in the morning one day a week and drive to the schools. They park in the parking lot and pray for that school, the principal, teachers, and students, then drive on to the next school and pray the same way.

Another author tells how she spends much time in prayer and searching the Bible for just the right scripture for each member of her family. Then she prays this text for them daily. The verse becomes very special to the person for whom it was chosen.

The friend who introduced me to sanctuary prayer (one of the greatest blessings of my spiritual life, by the way) often uses the steps of the sanctuary to pray individually for persons for whom she is especially burdened, praying at the altar of sacrifice for the forgiveness of their sins, at the laver for their cleansing, at the lampstand for the complete involvement of the Holy Spirit in their life; praying that they may hunger and thirst for God at the table of shewbread and finally holding them up in intercession at the altar of incense. Just exactly what she prays for at each step, of course, differs each time, but it offers an idea of how it works. She has some tremendous stories of how God has led in the lives of the people she has prayed for this way.

My suggestion is to vary your prayer life. It is so easy to fall into a rut, until prayer becomes a burden. Although you may always want to have your morning devotions in the same place at the same time, you can vary your intercession time. Praying throughout the day may be a very good idea for many of you. Also, using daily prayer lists makes it easier and more manageable.

Some people like to write their prayers. But it seems to me that it would limit how many people you could pray for, as it takes so long to write. But it is helpful to keep a spiritual diary of those on your innermost list—close family and friends—and the prayers you offer for them.

Another idea I really like is to take a day when you can be alone for the greater portion of time—either at home or somewhere where you can go to be by yourself—and make a special retreat of intercession, praying either for your whole list or a special portion that you have chosen. It can also be a day of fasting for you, or you can bring along a simple lunch to eat. Take your Bible and perhaps some other devotional book (such as *The Desire of Ages*), and spend some of your time reading. I really like this idea and want to put it into practice regularly—maybe once a month.

Another variation of this retreat is to ask two or three friends to join you in a time of special intercession for specific people or missions and to pray in much the same way.

A shorter version would be to maybe once a week set aside one or two hours in a mini retreat of intercession.

You can divide prayer lists into sections by families, topics, places, or interests, thus making it easier to pray intelligently for the people on your list.

One of the things I have discovered about God is that He values our intelligence, our creativity, our earnestness, and our honesty. Any use of these ideas to earn brownie points for the kingdom will be useless. But any sincere reaching out to God in intercession for others He will value much more than we have any idea of, no matter how we choose to express ourselves. We can *sing* our prayers or go out into a mountain meadow where no one can hear and *shout* them. God will listen and answer. (He may also smile!)

Christ's parable of the poor man who had nothing to give his friend and so asked his rich neighbor for bread reveals the marks of a true intercessor. It isn't *how* we pray, or even *when,* but the qualities

shown by the parable:
"A sense of the need of souls,
a Christlike love in the heart,
a consciousness of personal impotence,
faith in the power of prayer,
courage to persevere in spite of refusal,
and the assurance of an abundant reward.
"These are the qualities that change a Christian into an intercessor and call forth the power of prevailing prayer" (Murray, *The
Ministry of Intercessory Prayer,* p. 40).

SUMMARY

Although the Spirit plants the desire to pray in the heart of every
born-again Christian, sometimes we need instruction and guidance
in *how* to pray. We need enough structure to make it easy for us to
understand what the goals of our prayer are so that we can recognize
God's answers to it. This in turn will build our faith and make it easy
for us to remember to pray.

Here are a few suggestions on how to begin a personal ministry of
intercession.

Whom to pray for: Select from the following three divisions:

1. Family, friends, neighbors, business and social acquaintances.

2. The work of God: individual congregations, pastors, evangelists, etc.

3. World leadership: presidents and other leaders, governments,
etc.

Begin small and be specific. Add to your list as God impresses you.

Why intercession is important: Our prayers allow God to do for
others what He could not do if we did not pray.

What we can ask God to do for others: We can ask God's blessing
on all those on our prayer list. However, God will sometimes give us
specific Bible texts to use in our prayers for individuals. Jot them
down next to their name. Or we can ask the people themselves what

they want us to pray about. Anything that God promises to give His people is an appropriate prayer: salvation, victory over sin, forgiveness of sin, boldness in witness, the fruit of the Spirit, power in prayer, good health, a sound mind. We can pray for students to be diligent in studies and earn good grades. Or we can pray that others will make good choices of careers, jobs, or the right marriage partners. Always conclude with "Thy will be done." Only God knows the end from the beginning and what is best for each person.

When to intercede for others: Intercession can be a part of your daily morning devotions or a separate prayer time, or divided into several segments throughout the day. Whenever possible we need to know the people on our lists well enough to know the specific problems they are facing and then pray for them about these at the appropriate times.

Where and how to pray: Posture is important only in that our hearts should be bowed at the footstool of the King of kings. Intercession can be done alone, in the family, or in a small group.

Take a personal prayer retreat, either most of the day or just an hour or two—either alone or with a friend. Vary your prayer life both to avoid falling into a rut and to keep it exciting.

God will value any sincere reaching out to Him in intercession no matter how we choose to express ourselves. Sing, shout, whisper, write. God will hear and answer.

Chapter Ten

WHEN GOD ANSWERS

W E ALL LIKE TO SEE RESULTS. It is the only way we have to evaluate whether we are on the right track, to decide if what we are doing is profitable. The same applies to prayer. We need to *see* some answers to be sure that we are praying correctly and effectively.

How can you tell if God is responding to your prayers? We have all read stories of answers to prayer that thrill our hearts, and we love to hear how God dramatically intervenes in lives of people because of the prayers of other people. All of us long to pray such prayers. But if we are honest, we will most likely admit that it seldom happens that way for us. Oh, yes, perhaps we have a couple of favorite stories we eagerly share. But we pray every day. What happens to the rest of our prayers?

Although we grimly hold on in faith, many of us secretly doubt that we're really worthy of God answering our prayers. Wouldn't it be wonderful if we could find a way to open up a dialogue between us and God in which we could discuss this with Him and He could correct our prayers if need be and give us a small glimpse of His response to them? I realize that the ultimate goal of the born-again Christian is to have such great faith that we can always rest in the confidence that God is answering our prayers. However, who among us can always be sure that we understand God fully? Sometimes my prayers need to be corrected. That's the human part of prayer. So I need some way of asking God if I am praying in His will.

Prayer is meant to be answered. God delights to respond to our prayers. Scriptures radiate certainty that God is eager to fulfill them. But I have sometimes wondered over the discrepancy between what God wants to do and what seems to happen in our experience. Could it be that the problem is often in our spiritual eyesight, that we don't recognize His answers? Is it possible that God is willing to teach us how to view things as He does and so be able to discern Him at work? That we can learn to see through the darkness?

Many of the prayers we pray for others God can accomplish only as a matter of *their* spiritual growth. What we long most for those we love is that they will be saved in God's kingdom. But salvation can never be granted against the free will of the person involved. If, when I prayed, God intervened in a person's life to change thoughts and actions against the person's will, He would be manipulative and encroach upon personal freedom. What God does is to set up or allow a series of events, possible because of my prayers, that will cause the person to stop and think, and gradually his or her thoughts and actions change subject, of course, to the person's individual choices.

GOD ANSWERS PRAYER *TODAY*

The most important condition to answered prayer is faith—believing that God means it when He says that He answers every heartfelt prayer. If we have not prayed haphazardly, but under the direction of the Holy Spirit, God will fulfill them. The Bible is very positive about this. Answered, not tomorrow, not next month, but today. *Today* God is answering my prayer.

> I was regretting the past
> and fearing the future.
> Suddenly God was speaking,
> "MY NAME IS 'I AM.' "
> I waited. God continued:
> "When you live in the past
> with its mistakes and regrets,
> it is hard. I am not there.
> MY NAME IS NOT 'I WAS.'
> When you live in the future
> with its problems and fears,

it is hard. I am not there.
My name is not 'I WILL BE.'
When you live in this moment,
it is not hard. I am here.
MY NAME IS 'I AM.' "

—Plaque on the wall of the guesthouse kitchen, St. Benedict's Monastery, Snowmass, Colorado (in *Guideposts,* June 1994).

I may not see the answer for many days, but the angels are busy today answering my prayers, sometimes bit by bit—always honoring human freedom—but they are at work. According to Scripture, every prayer is heard and answered.

It's hard to hold on to belief when our physical sight seems to bear out just the opposite. Fortunately, God is gracious and willing to encourage us along until faith takes hold. He understands our humanity. But if we want to be faithful and consistent intercessors, we need to comprehend this truth. It is impossible to continue to pray in faith every day for people if you are not sure that God is answering because of the lack of physical evidence.

I have sometimes questioned if God was really answering some of my prayers for individuals. Oh, I believed He was—intellectually. But sometimes my heart wavered a bit. I couldn't see anything happening. However, God has always been willing to give me assurances when I need them.

Remember my story of little faith and great faith. Little faith, when met with trials, tries frantically to find solutions. At last, in desperation, little faith turns to God for help. Great faith, on the other hand, in any problem, turns immediately to God. I believe the faith family has still another member—*growing faith.* That is who I am. And most likely, you too. And God is willing to strengthen our growing faith by giving us assurances along the way of His constant care. As our faith grows, more and more we will be able to trust Him completely, even when we cannot see. Then one day we will have great faith.

In my growing faith I sometimes need to stop and check with God to see if I am praying in His will. Not to test God, but to test myself. When I receive His assurance, then I can pray on though seeing no apparent change in circumstances, but praying in faith that God is working on the problem.

The psalmist David so often helps me in trusting God. David says that there are two things about God that he is sure of: "One thing God has spoken, two things have I heard: that you, O God, are strong, and that you, O Lord, are loving" (Ps. 62:11, 12).

Those two things help me greatly in entrusting those I love into the hands of God. God is so strong that He can do anything. Nothing is impossible for Him. But not only is God strong; He is also loving. In His power and strength He will always do the loving thing. That covers everything I could desire in a God. And how it builds my faith!

One Thursday night just before Mother's Day, I knelt beside my bed and discussed my children with God. My heart grieved for my oldest son, John, Jr., as he had left his belief in God behind him as he had grown into manhood. I had been praying for him continually, yet could see no change in his attitude toward God or toward us. Oh, John was always loving toward his father and me. But he lived in a world apart from the rest of his family. He came home occasionally for Thanksgiving or Christmas—if it was convenient and if we begged him to. But his world had no birthdays, no Mother's Days, no Father's Days. In all the years he had lived apart from us he had never sent me a Mother's Day card or called to wish me a happy Mother's Day. And so as I faced another Mother's Day I realized that it was unlikely that the coming holiday would be any different. I would hear from the other three children, but not from him.

My heart seemed ready to break. How much longer could I handle this waiting and seeing nothing? Without even realizing it, a prayer burst forth from my lips.

"O, Lord," I cried, "I just feel I have to have some sort of assurance from You that You are really at work in my son's life. I see nothing changing. Oh, it would be so nice if some way I could either have someone call me and tell me something encouraging about him or if he could just call and wish me a happy Mother's Day. Either thing sounds improbable, but if You could possibly arrange one of them for me, it would be the best Mother's Day present I have ever received! And then I could know beyond the shadow of a doubt that You are at work in my son's life and that in Your timing he will return to You."

It was the first time in my life I had ever dared to offer such a prayer. As I paused and considered what I had just asked of God, I began to be fearful that it was a presumptuous prayer and showed a lack of faith. So I prayed on:

"I don't mean to be presumptuous, Father. If this is an improper prayer, please forget I prayed it. I won't love You any less because You don't answer it." But then the longing to receive assurance about my son filled my heart again, and almost against my will I cried out, "But, oh, if You could possibly answer it, I'd love it! It would make me so happy."

I approached that Mother's Day with wary anticipation. I had never prayed like this before. Would God answer?

My daughter was the only child living at home at the time. When Julie and I arrived home from work and school on Friday afternoon, I found numerous little Mother's Day surprises that my husband had planned for me. Roses in the kitchen and on the dining room table, and even a lavender vase with a single rose in my bathroom. The refrigerator held a huge bowl of sweetened strawberries just ready to be spooned into a bowl to eat. My favorite flower and my favorite fruit! Cards from my daughter and my husband lay on the table.

The Sabbath mail brought cards from my two younger sons assuring me of their love and their remembrances of me on this special day. Sunday dawned bright and beautiful, and I busied myself around the house with my regular Sunday chores. Working five days a week away from home meant that Sunday was a day to catch up on the washing, the ironing, and the mending. The telephone was silent.

Toward evening my husband persuaded me to go out to eat with him. Julie opted to stay home and get ready for school the next day.

"You had a telephone call," she greeted me when I arrived home. My heart leaped. John?

"It was Tom," Julie said. "He wanted to talk to you in person to wish you a happy Mother's Day even though he had already sent a card. Too bad you weren't here to talk to him."

My fluttering heart subsided, and I sighed. It was very nice that my youngest son was thinking of me. But one son cannot take the place of another.

I was getting ready for bed when the phone rang again. My hand reached out weakly for the phone.

"Hello," I said.

"Hello, Mom," a voice responded cheerily. "Happy Mother's Day!"

I was almost too excited to speak. It was John. God had answered my prayer, and John had remembered me on this special day. My son loved me. But even more, I realized that God loved me so much that He was willing to strengthen my weak faith with this assurance. How like God, the loving Father!

In my excitement I told John of my prayer and how delighted I was to hear from him. The interesting aftermath of this was that for the next several years John called me every Mother's Day. So each year God said to me through those calls, "See, I am still at work in John's life." One year I arrived home from church on Sabbath and found a florist's bouquet on my doorstep. John had sent me flowers for Mother's Day! Unheard of. How I praised God. One prayer and so many answers.

But then my son slipped back into his world of no holidays and has remained there ever since. But I know—oh, yes, I know—God is working in his life and answering my prayers. Someday, if not here on earth, then in heaven, I will be able to look at God's records and see the intense activity on behalf of my son.

I believe that it is God's will that we trust Him completely without noticing results. But I also think that God understands our human need of sometimes seeing something with our own eyes. I think of John the Baptist as he languished in prison and began to wonder why Jesus did not come to his defense. Was Jesus really the Christ? John sent his disciples to ask Him.

"Stay here today," Jesus told them, "and see what I do. Then go and tell John what you saw."

The crowd thronged around Jesus all day, and John's disciples watched intently as He healed the sick, cast out demons, and taught the people. They marveled at His power and took the clear message back to John: "Jesus is the Christ." God honored him by patiently spelling out truth when his faith wavered.

I am not suggesting that we often ask God to show us that He is at work. Our faith should assure us of that. But sometimes the Holy Spirit will put into our hearts a prayer of desperate longing for confidence that we are praying in His will. We should never stifle that prayer, but trust God enough to give it expression. What Jesus did for John the Baptist, God will do for us—reveal His power. And when we see His power, we can more fully trust Him for the outcome.

Another time the Holy Spirit planted this same type of prayer in my heart. This was soon after I had begun my structured intercessory prayer ministry. To be truthful, I expected that when I stepped out in faith to pray aggressively for others, God would send some pretty exciting answers. But it didn't work that way. Things seemed to go on just as they had before. I began to wonder if perhaps I had misunderstood His plans for my life. So I asked Him if He would affirm the call to a ministry of intercession by letting me *see* the answer to at least one of my prayers.

One of the women I was praying for was Cheryl, a friend of mine from grade school days. We weren't close friends, but we had kept in touch over the years. Just recently I had heard that she had been suffering from depression for a period of several years, so I was praying especially about this. I knew that it is not God's desire that a Christian remain in depression. One day Cheryl called me and said that she and her husband would be in our area on a Maranatha mission and wondered if we could get together. So I invited the couple to our house for Sabbath dinner.

The day turned out cold and wet, rain turned into sleet in our mountains, and then into snow. I was fearful that the stormy weather would discourage Cheryl and her husband from braving our winding mountain roads. But they came. Her husband laughed at the rain and snow, assuring us that they were used to much worse. We dried them out in front of our woodstove, fed them hot vegetable soup and cornbread, and enjoyed sweet fellowship around the table. After dinner the two men collapsed on the couches for a little nap, and Cheryl and I renewed our friendship as we sat by the fire and watched the snowflakes drifting down outside. We talked about our children, our lives, and our dreams—sharing in a way we had never had the opportunity to do before.

As they were preparing to leave to go down the mountain before darkness made the driving hazardous, Cheryl turned to me and asked abruptly, "Do you know that I have been in depression?"

I was hesitant to answer, wondering if perhaps she hadn't wanted me to know.

"Yes," I answered, then quickly added, "I've been praying for you especially about that."

"I knew you were," came her surprising response. "I've felt your prayers. My depression is gone."

A quick hug and a prayer later, Cheryl and her husband whirled out of my life again. But not out of my prayers. I continue to pray for Cheryl, her sons, her husband, her marriage, and her relationship with God.

Not a dramatic answer to my prayer—but a glimpse into God's work in answer to my prayers for Cheryl. It was as though God was

saying, "Do not doubt that I have called you to a ministry of intercession. You may not hear about any immediate results, but your
prayers are constantly being answered. Pray on in faith."

I have discovered five ways to take a more positive approach toward God in my prayer ministry. First, I cultivate a spirit of thankfulness in my heart for God's work in the lives of those I am praying for.
Second, I look for any visible improvement in their lives—spiritual,
physical, or financial—and specifically thank God for it. The third way
is to realize that I do not always know how to pray. I do not know the
real needs of the people, but the Holy Spirit always does. Much of my
prayer list is a "God bless" list, just trusting my people wholly to God
to lead them to salvation, health, and joy in Christ. Sometimes God
impresses me of specific things to pray for or about, special promises
to claim. I do so with joy, thanking God for this additional involvement in prayer.

Fourth, I ask the Lord to give me more love for the people I pray
for, more intensity of desire in my prayers. I want it to matter to me
what happens to those whom the Lord has entrusted me to pray for.
Sometimes the hunger, hurt, and violence of the world around us
deadens our caring. I don't want that to be true of me. The *only*
prayers that God can honestly answer are those that come from the
heart. If I don't really care, it is useless to pretend with God.

The fifth way I make my prayer ministry more positive is to *act* in
concert with prayer. I write letters, make telephone calls, and visit
when it is appropriate—and possible. I make remembrances of all
kinds. For many people a note of encouragement or a telephone call
immeasurably brightens their day. Let's train ourselves to reach out to
humanity around us. So many people wonder if anyone at all cares.
For our own encouragement it is wise to keep a prayer journal listing
how God is working in the lives of those on our prayer lists. It is easy
to forget the Lord's blessings if we do not write them down!

I can't tell you *how* God is going to answer your prayers. But I can
tell you that He *is* answering them. "This is the confidence we have in

approaching God: that if we ask anything according to his will, he hears us. And if we know that he hears us—whatever we ask—we know that we have what we asked of him" (1 John 5:14, 15).

WHAT INTERCESSION CAN DO

Intercession changes and blesses the subjects of our intercession, but perhaps the person interceding receives the greater blessing.

Possibly you have read Ellen White's story of a man caught in a snowstorm while traveling. Struggling through the deep drifts of snow, chilled and exhausted, he doubted his ability to go on. Just as he was about to abandon all thoughts of reaching shelter and to yield to the temptation to sink down into the softness of the snow, he heard the cries and moans of a fellow traveler who had been unable to go on. Immediately aroused to help him, the first man struggled through the snow until he found the other. He massaged his frozen limbs, raised him to his feet, and when he found the man could not walk, he carried him through the very drifts that a short while before he had felt he could not manage alone. He finally made it through the storm to a shelter where both he and the stranger were thawed out and fed. As he sat by the fire, it dawned on him that in saving this man he had saved himself (see *Testimonies*, vol. 4, p. 319).

Her story describes the role of an intercessor. Intercessors are not those who have it all together. Rather, they are those who are struggling themselves yet, hearing the cries of humanity around them, carry the dying ones to shelter through their prayers. And in the kingdom the intercessors will find that in praying for others they saved their own lives.

In this book you hear me emphasizing prayer for others. I do not mean to stress prayer over service. Jesus surely never did. But more books have been written about how to work for the Lord than on how to pray and wait. We need training in prayer. Service without prayer will accomplish little. And some situations tie our hands as far as service is concerned, leaving prayer the only option.

Somewhere I read the story of a city in England and a dying church. The pastor had called in evangelists for crusades, but apathy reigned. They had little response to altar calls. One member of the church was an elderly woman unable to leave her home, but who felt a great burden for revival in her congregation. One day she read in a church paper of the work of Dwight L. Moody in the United States and his powerful revivals. Impressed to pray that Moody would come to her church, she prayed with this in mind for several years. Then one day her brother returned home from a church meeting with a strange light in his face.

"You won't believe, sister," he said, "what happened at church today."

"Tell me," she asked eagerly.

"A minister from the United States spoke," her brother replied, "and when he gave a call at the close of the service, half the congregation went forward. The pastor has asked him to stay and hold revival services."

"What is the minister's name?"

"Dwight Moody," the brother answered.

Through the prayers of that one elderly housebound woman a revival began that stirred all England.

What can intercession do? It can bring about revival. Intercession can hold up the weary hands of pastors, missionaries, and evangelists in their work, and give new life to the careless and discouraged. Most of all, it can save a church, a family, or a friend.

SUMMARY

God delights to answer our prayers. Scripture radiates certainty that God is eager to answer them. Then why is it that we see so few answers to our prayers?

We need to cultivate spiritual eyesight so that we can recognize God's answers. Spiritual eyesight includes remembering:

1. God values individual freedom and never intervenes against the person's will.

2. God is at work answering my prayer *today*, although I may not see the completed answer for many days.

3. God is willing to give us assurances along the way that He is answering our prayers.

4. The faith family has three members: *little faith*, *great faith*, and *growing faith*. Most of us are growing faith.

Two things to remember about God: (1) He is *strong*—able to do the humanly impossible, and (2) He will always do the *loving* thing.

Five ways I have discovered that enable you to take a more positive approach toward God about intercession:

1. Cultivate a spirit of thankfulness for God's work in the lives of those you pray for.

2. Thank God for any visible improvement in the lives of those you are praying for.

3. Realize that although you do not always know how to pray for your people, you can trust God to bless them. At the same time, listen for God's impressions of specific things to pray for.

4. Ask the Lord to give you more love for the people you pray for, more intensity of desire.

5. *Act* in concert with your prayers—writing letters, telephoning, visiting. Maintain a prayer journal listing how God is working in the lives of those you pray for, to keep your memories of God's blessings fresh.

Intercession works two ways. It changes and blesses the subjects of our intercession, but perhaps the person interceding receives the greater blessing.

Prayer should not be emphasized over service, yet service without prayer will accomplish little.

What can intercession do? It can bring about revival and hold up the weary hands of pastors, missionaries, and evangelists in their work. Giving new life to the careless and discouraged, it can save a church, a family, or a friend.

AM I MY BROTHER'S KEEPER?

AIN'S QUESTION "Am I my brother's keeper?" is still pertinent today. And the lawyer's query "Who is my neighbor?" reaches out further yet. A whole needy world out there clamors for our attention.

But we are each only one person, limited by human weakness. We can't satisfy even the needs of our immediate families, much less those of the world! How can we bear to contemplate the misery of the world without dying ourselves of pain and hopelessness? Only *in Christ* is there hope, balm for every pain. Jesus can fill every heart's desire. And He has asked *us* to be the hand reaching out to Him through prayer for the world.

Why is human intercession necessary? Isn't God already doing everything possible for the world? What have we got to do with it?

Satan still claims the world as his because of human rebellion. Since part of God's inherent character is freedom, He will never force humanity to obey Him. He leaves us free to choose whom we will serve—God or Satan. Because of our freedom, God will not arbitrarily step into any person's life, since to do so would violate the law of freedom. Satan would be quick to shout, "Not fair!" Yet Satan also knows that before the entrance of sin, God had created human hearts with the desire and ability to reach out to God and ask for blessings for the world. Sin alone made human beings totally self-serving. The new-birth experience re-creates this original desire and ability in us. Satan knows that he cannot charge Jesus with taking unfair advantage when He answers our prayers for others, since it was part of the Creator's original plan. The devil understands more than most Christians do the power of intercessory prayer. Our prayers totally silence his accusations and give God the opportunity to work in behalf of many who might never have sought Him without our prayers.

Because Cain had rebelled against God, he also rebelled against his brother, ignoring his responsibility to love and protect him. But as Christians our hearts are once again in tune with God's and thus open to the needs of humanity around us. It is only *in Christ* that we can open ourselves to such hurt. And it is only *in Christ* that we can intercede.

We can have no greater privilege than intercession, to bring before Him the needs of another with deep heart longing and love. When Jesus chose us as His younger brother or sister, He chose us for this very work—to join Him in interceding for the world.

It is seldom that the prayers of one person stand alone. Almost always—perhaps always—the Holy Spirit places the same prayer upon the hearts of numerous people. The story I am about to tell involved the prayers of many people.

My younger son, Tom, had a desire to raise his children as Seventh-day Adventist Christians. Yet over the years he allowed worry, overwork, and lack of time to dim his relationship with God to the point that he sometimes even doubted God's very existence. These negative emotions tainted the lives of his children and colored all his relationships.

Gradually Tom began to realize that something of vital importance was missing from his life, and he desired to change. His family decided to attend Redwood camp meeting last summer. My husband and I rejoiced as we heard that news! We prayed that God would send the very messages Tom needed to hear. Typical mother that I am, I urged my son to attend every meeting!

"Well, you know how hard it is for me to sit still," Tom told me, "but if I get too bored, I'll just take the kids and run over to the beach."

Dismay filled my thoughts, and I began new prayers.

"Oh, Lord, don't let Tom take the children away from their meetings to go to the beach," I prayed. "Let there be something at camp meeting that fills his emptiness. May the whole family be blessed."

God answered those prayers abundantly. Pastor Steven Wallace presented a series of lectures on character development that changed Tom's complete focus and gave him new hope for a victorious life. By November, when Tom and his family visited us for the Thanksgiving holiday, the change was apparent. In the past our daughter-in-law, Judy, had carried the whole load of conducting family worship. I had often regretted that my grandchildren did not enjoy singing for worships as our own children had. But now what a reversal! Tom led his children in singing, while both he and his 10-year-old son, Tommy, accompanied on guitars. And how the children sang! They nearly raised the roof! The 6-year-old belted out his favorite songs, and everyone sang with enthusiasm, suggesting more and more favorite songs. It was hard to stop the singing. When Judy read from a simplified version of *The Story of Redemption,* by Ellen White, the children listened attentively. I marveled at God's abundant answer. Tom was walking in newness of life, the children sang, his son Tommy had learned to play the guitar, and a new joy possessed the whole family.

In April my husband and I visited this family in their own home. The now-11-year-old Tommy had asked his grandfather to baptize him, and the date was set for the first Sabbath we were there. On the Friday night before his baptism we were pleased with how well Tommy was progressing with his music. His guitar playing for worship was almost professional. We found out he had already played a guitar duet with his father for adult Sabbath school and often accompanied Pathfinder and junior Sabbath school song services. His developing abilities gave the boy a new maturity and confidence.

When our son Tom came downstairs the Sabbath morning of the baptism, he asked me, "Mom, did you suggest that Tommy write notes of appreciation to Judy and me?"

"No," I said, "I don't know anything about any notes."

"When Judy and I went up to our bedroom last night, we each found a note on our nightstand," he said. "It amazed me. I wondered if you had put Tommy up to it."

I reiterated my ignorance. "What did the notes say?" I asked.

It seemed hard for Tom to speak, but at last he got the words out. "Tommy said, 'When you changed, Dad, I changed too.' "

As my heart responded with thanksgiving and joy, I remembered that God's promises were not only to us, but to our children and their children, down through the generations.

The baptism was in an outdoor baptistry. As Tommy and his grandfather stood barefooted in their white robes, the blue sky and the sun overhead, the pool below, my husband gave the church members the opportunity to say a word about Tommy just before the baptism. Tommy's maternal grandfather, his Pathfinder leader, his Sabbath school teacher, and others mentioned things they had appreciated about the boy. Then Grandpa asked Tommy if the influence of anyone special had led to his making the decision to be baptized.

"Yeah," Tommy said, "my dad."

No doubt a citywide revival is a glorious blessing. But for me, the revival of one son and grandson constituted all I could hold of happiness.

God took a great chance when He gave humanity the responsibility of intercession. But He took it because He foresaw that it was the very best way to prepare a world—and the universe—for eternal salvation.

Fatma